Pots de Fleurs

By Kathy Delaney

Editor: Judy Pearlstein
Designer: Kelly Ludwig
Photography: Aaron T. Leimkuehler
Illustration: Kathy Delaney and Lon Eric Craven
Technical Editor: Christina DeArmond
Production assistance: Jo Ann Groves

Published by: Kansas City Star Books
1729 Grand Blvd.
Kansas City, Missouri, USA 64108

First edition, first printing
ISBN: 978-1-933466-80-4
Library of Congress Control Number: 2008942686
Printed in the United States of America by Walsworth
Publishing Co., Marceline, MO

To order copies, call StarInfo at (816) 234-4636 and say
"Books."

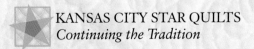

KANSAS CITY STAR QUILTS
Continuing the Tradition

PickleDish.com
The Quilter's Home Page

www.PickleDish.com

Acknowledgements

A garden takes many levels of contribution to bloom
successfully. A book is very much like a garden.
Someone begins by preparing the land – thank you,
Doug Weaver, for your confidence in me that you let
me share what I love through my books.

The garden also needs someone to oversee the
watering and weeding. Judy Pearlstein, once
again you keep me focused. Thank you for all your
help in creating my books. And thank you, Aaron
Leimkuehler, for the wonderful studio photographs, Jo
Ann Groves for making my instructional photographs
look so good, Eric Craven for making my drawings
look so great and Christina DeArmond for keeping the
numbers correct.

Every beautiful garden also needs an architect who
takes the vision and creates the beautiful beds and
paths. Kelly Ludwig, thank you so much for making
this such a beautiful book!

But it's the seeds that are planted that truly make the
garden bloom. Thank you so very much to the quilters
who took my patterns and made such wonderful
samples for the gallery. Without you, this book could
not have been made! Thank you Kelly Ashton, Barb
Fife, Karen G. Fisher, Pearle Gerdes, Sandy Gore, Tresa
Jones, Nancy Kerns, Linda Mooney, Carol Nash, Mindy
Peterson, Freda Smith, Karen Thompson, Eugena
Turner, and Susan Winnie.

Pots de Fleurs

A Garden of Applique Techniques

by Kathy Delaney

About the Author

Kathy cannot remember when she wasn't sewing. Starting with doll clothes and graduating to her own clothes when she was ten, Kathy has had a love affair with fabric that has never diminished.

Since meeting her first quilt in 1991, Kathy has moved away from clothing almost entirely and has devoted her creative endeavors to the making of quilts. In fact, on any given day, she can be found thinking about her next quilt, shopping for fabric for a new quilt, stitching on a current quilt, writing about quiltmaking techniques, designing patterns for quilters, sketching ideas for another appliqué quilt, taking a workshop to learn a new technique, attending a guild meeting, lecturing or teaching quiltmaking techniques, appliqué being her favorite. In fact, her husband does not believe she does anything but make quilts. He just might be right!

Kathy lives in Overland Park, Kansas with Rich, her husband of nearly 37 years. She and her husband have two sons, Sean, 28, a former Captain in the United States Army, and Ian, 24, an actor living in North Hollywood. Kathy and Rich also are proud grandparents of two-year old twins, born to Sean and his wife Alicia.

Kathy has appeared on "Simply Quilts with Alex Anderson" on HGTV and teaches nationally and internationally. Kathy is available to travel for guild programs, workshops and judging. She may be contacted through her website, www.kathydelaney.com.

Contents

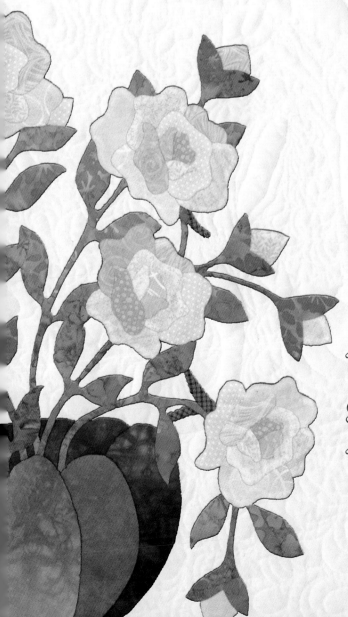

Introduction

I don't think there is any more relaxing activity than handwork. And my favorite handwork is hand appliqué. If I'm feeling stressed or anxious, picking up an appliqué block seems to just calm me and raise my spirits like nothing else — even chocolate. When I finish a major project, I tend to pace around for a bit until I get a new project started. Hand appliqué makes me happy! And so far, appliqué has not made me gain weight like chocolate has!

As a teacher of quiltmaking techniques, I am very passionate about teaching, but most passionate about teaching appliqué. I just know that you'll find the same peace, happiness and satisfaction in appliqué I do if you just give it a chance. So, on the following pages you will find what I hope you'll think is a great design to entice you into trying the various techniques I will be presenting and a technique or two to help you accomplish anything appliqué.

My goal is to provide a number of opportunities to find the technique(s) that will make appliqué easy for you. By trying the various methods, I am hoping you will discover several truths. First, appliqué is not a dirty word! It is a technique that accomplishes beautiful quilts. It even lets you do more than you might otherwise as hand appliqué is so very portable. You can do it anywhere!

Second, I want you to discover, as I have, there is no one way to do anything when it comes to quilt making. Some of the techniques I will be presenting will work best with some projects while others will work better with other designs. I believe the more you know, the easier the whole process becomes. Each of us has different skill levels. I'm hoping the tips and techniques I present within these pages will help you find what works best for you.

So, are you ready for an adventure? We're going to have some fun together, so let's get started!

Supplies Used in Hand Appliqué

⊰ Fabric

While you can appliqué with any fabric, 100% cotton tends to be the easiest when employing the needleturn technique. While a cotton-poly blend could give you somewhat the same look as 100% cotton, the polyester in the blend will fight you as you try to turn the seam allowance with your needle. I don't think it is worth the trouble!

I am often asked if one should wash the fabric before use. Some stitchers actually like the feel of the fabric AFTER washing. The sizing is removed as well as the excess dye so the fabric usually has a softer hand. Some stitchers seem to think the fabric is easier to work with after washing. I've even heard some voice their concerns about handling the chemicals in the fabric like formaldehyde, so washing first is important to them to remove as much as possible. Other stitchers prefer the sizing be left in. They feel the stability offered by the sizing makes the appliqué easier to work with.

I will be honest — I don't always wash my fabric. I will test a suspected fabric for bleeding and wash or not accordingly, but I don't always wash. That said, let me tell you of a horrible experience that has absolutely nothing to do with bleeding. When I made the quilt "Horn of Plenty for a New Century" for my book by the same name (Kansas City Star Books, 2004), I did not wash the background fabric. I used a lot of batik and hand-dyed fabrics (some I dyed myself) and happily stitched the appliqué to my background blocks. When it came time to mark

the finished top for quilting, I tested three markers in an attempt to find the perfect marker, one that would wash out easily. (I know, but hope springs eternal!)

Using an extra background block from the quilt, I sprayed starch on the top half. I had heard someplace that if you heavily starch your quilt top before marking for quilting, you will be marking the starch more than the fabric, letting the marker wash out easily after the quilting was finished. I tested three different markers by writing their brand names, first on the starched half and then again on the untreated half. After washing in the machine as I planned to wash the finished quilt, and then drying in the clothes drier, I found two very disturbing things. First, all six written samples of the markers were clearly still evident! Clearly, the starch had no impact on these so-called washable markers. Second, and most disturbing, the 9 1/2" by 12 1/2" fabric block had shrunk 3/4" in one direction and a full inch in the other.

I am positive the appliqué fabrics will not shrink that much if I were to wash my finished quilt. Consequently, if I don't want to ruin what is to me a valuable quilt, I can never wash it. Now, while I may not automatically wash my fabrics for appliqué, I will at the very least test for shrinkage!

❧ Thread

We are so lucky today! Our quilt supply shops are teaming with wonderful confections in the guise of fabric and threads. When you are appliquéing by hand, match the thread to the appliqué fabric. There are a variety of fibers and brands on the market.

Most stitchers will stitch with 100% cotton. There is a huge segment of the appliquéing population who stitch with 100% silk. There are even very fine polyester threads. Whichever you prefer, I recommend the thread match the color of the appliqué fabric. I like my stitches to be as invisible as possible. If the thread matches the fabric, the stitches blend into the fabric. So, even if I have been less than skillful in my execution, the stitches are hidden in plain sight. I know there are stitchers who use just six colors of thread; black, white, cream, taupe, camel and charcoal. When I tried stitching exclusively with the six colors though, no matter

how careful I was, I could not hide my stitches as well as when I match the thread to the appliqué fabric.

Whatever you decide, color wise, I recommend using as thin a thread as possible. A strong, long-staple 2-ply, 60 wt. cotton thread or a 50 wt. silk thread (or even a #100) is likely to blend with your appliqué fabric. Sewing small stitches, close together, will make your appliqué secure. This thinner thread will also let you use a very fine needle. Any heftier a thread and you will have trouble threading the needle.

There are a variety of thread brands on the market. Experiment to see which one you like the best.

❧ Needles

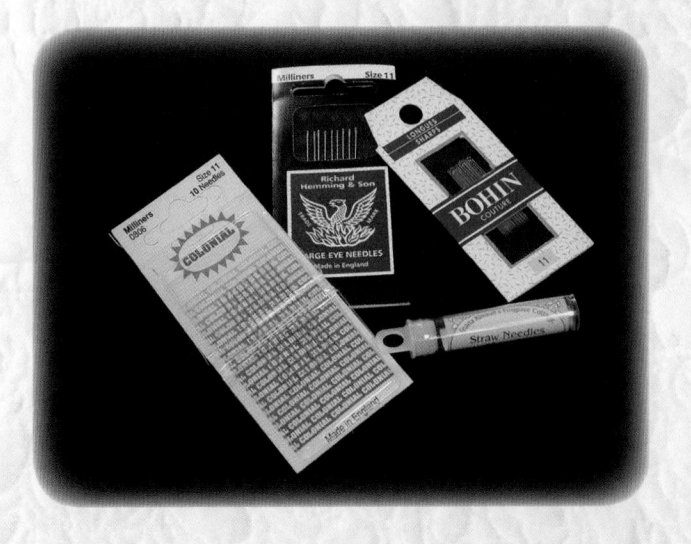

It seems that there are different needles for every stitching activity. So many choices! You can actually stitch appliqué with several different needles. I know of some fabulous appliqué artists who stitch with a very short quilting Between! I can't even hold that short a needle, let alone guide it with any skill to stitch with it! Most people tend to stitch with the traditional needle of choice, the Sharp. It's a little longer than the Between. I found it to be short enough that the end of the needle hit the same spot on my finger with every stitch and it just got exceedingly sore. So when I found the Straw, or Milliner needle, I discovered the longer length was the answer to my problem. I would recommend you try the different needles and find the one that works best for you.

It is my experience that a thinner needle will make the better stitch. I recommend the #11 or #12 Sharp or the #11 Straw/Milliner needles. The very fine wires from which these needles are fashioned let you make the finest of stitches. In addition, if you like to use Batik fabrics for your appliqué, the finer needle makes it easier stitching these very dense fabrics. Remember to use the very fine thread, though, so you won't have trouble threading the needle.

It is my philosophy that the finer the needle, the finer the thread, the finer the stitch!

✦ Scissors

Scissors for hand stitching are traditionally small — 4" embroidery scissors seem to work the best. To be comfortable, however, look for scissors that have large enough finger holes so as not to hinder your ease in manipulating the scissors. You will use them for cutting seam allowances as well as threads, so the traditional "stork scissors" might not be the best choice.

You will want scissors that are sharp all the way to the tip, a very narrow tip. The narrow, sharp tip is very important to my technique of making sharp points. Before purchasing scissors, it is a good idea to test them, so take some scrap fabric with you to the store. Make sure they are sharp, that the blades move freely and the contact point of the blades is true. It is amazing how difficult it is to even cut thread when the blades do not maintain contact throughout the cutting motion.

Markers

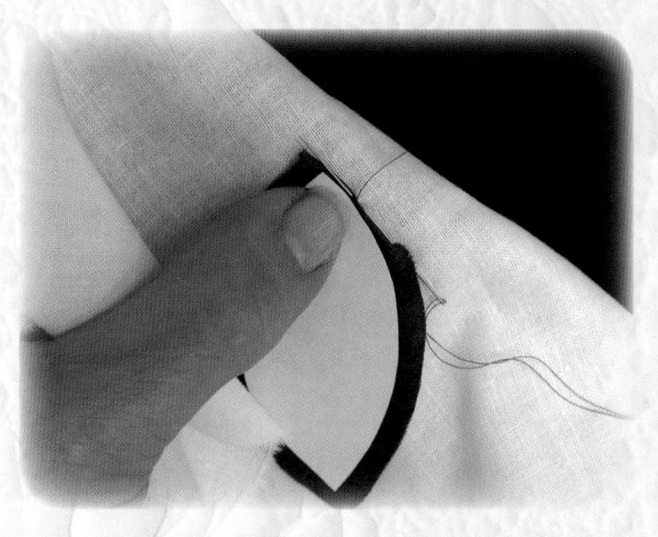

When preparing your appliqué pieces for stitching, you will need to make some decisions regarding how you'll know where the turn-under line is located. Some appliqué stitchers will attach the templates and use the edge of the template as their guide. I must admit, I really can't see what I'm doing and my stitches are definitely not hidden when I try to use the template as my guide. Even leaving the tiniest amount of fabric around a slightly smaller template doesn't work for me very well. (Try it — you may find it works great for you!)

Two things to remember; 1) the marks are part of the seam allowance and should not show on the finished appliqué, and 2) use a light marker on dark fabric or medium dark fabric, and a dark marker on light or medium light fabric.

There is a plethora of markers at your quilting supply store. For our purposes, almost any of them will work just fine with a few considerations. Color does matter. It has been my experience that a yellow, gray, light blue or pink marker is very hard to see on a medium fabric. I recommend using white or very dark on the medium fabric, testing to see which one actually works for the specific fabric.

Whether you use soapstone, chalk or one of the dressmaker pencils, it is advisable to begin with a newly sharpened point, especially if it has been in your notions drawer for some time. The "lead" of these markers will oxidize and form a skin over time. Once the skin forms, the marker's material will not transfer to your fabric. Sharpening the marker will eliminate the skin and then it will work fine.

ᔰ Template Materials

If you can draw on it, you can use it as a template. There is a long tradition for quiltmaking templates, be they for appliqué, patchwork or quilting designs, to be fashioned from found "paper" such as shirt cardboard, cereal box sides, manila folders or catalog covers. Today, quilters are fortunate to have at their fingertips modern template materials that are easy to work with and low in cost. Two of the most common are template plastic and freezer paper.

If I am stitching the same shape over and over, I will use the template plastic and make just one template. I use the one template to trace the shape directly onto the right side of my appliqué fabric. Sometimes I make the template a negative. That is, I use a craft knife and cut a "window" template. This lets me audition the fabric for my individual pieces. If you make a window template, be sure to make it slightly larger than you need to accommodate the turn-under line that you will trace within the window.

If I am stitching anything else, I use freezer paper for my templates. Most everyone can find rolls of freezer paper in their local grocery store. You can even find heavier precut sheets at your local quilting supply store that will easily go through your computer printer. I iron the freezer paper, waxy side down, to the right side of my appliqué fabric with a dry iron set on the wool setting. Then I trace the template with the appropriate marker and cut my seam allowances. I remove the freezer paper after placing the shape on the background and before stitching. The freezer paper stabilizes the fabric as it is positioned between the overlay and the background fabric. Once positioned, I pin the shape to the background with appliqué pins (very short pins) in the seam allowance, remove the freezer paper (slide a long pin or needle between paper and fabric to release the template without stretching the fabric), and reposition the pins into the interior of the shape and stitch.

ᔰ Sandpaper Board

When tracing the templates onto the right side of the appliqué fabric, you will find it easiest if the fabric does not move under the marker. Fine-grit sandpaper will hold the fabric still as you trace the template.

Your local quilt shop may have a manufactured sandpaper board available for purchase. But if not, you can make one. Simply glue a sheet of sandpaper to the inside of a file folder. You can get fancier by gluing the sandpaper sheet to a sturdier material — anything from poster board, a clip board or scrap Masonite board to a pre-glued linoleum floor tile. A board with a smooth side and the sandpaper side will even give you a lap board on which to work while sitting in an easy chair.

In a pinch, I have been known to place my appliqué fabric on top of another piece of fabric while I trace, as this works too.

Placement Techniques

Placing the appliqué pieces onto the background is one of the most crucial steps in appliqué. If you don't get everything placed correctly, according to the design, you may find the last pieces not fitting as they should. There are several methods to accomplish placement.

Marking the Background

The first method I learned for placing my appliqué pieces was marking the background with the design. Using a light box, I traced the design onto the right side of my background square with a marker that I could see. Placing the pattern onto the light box surface, I taped the pattern in place so it wouldn't move. Then I placed my background square over the pattern, aligning the center marks with a grid I created by folding the square in half in one direction and then in the other. I transferred the design to the fabric by tracing the pattern onto the right side of the fabric with a fabric marker.

When I placed my appliqué piece, I matched the outline of the shape to the outline marked onto the background square.

This could have worked just fine — it does for plenty of people — except for a few problems. First, my background was black. I found it very hard to see the black lines of the pattern as I was tracing through the black fabric. The second problem I encountered was my traced lines often were not covered by the appliqué. Somehow, my appliqué "crept" so the lines were left exposed or I didn't trace the shapes a tiny bit smaller so as to cover the lines.

Placement Overlay

I was very happy when I read an appliqué "how-to" book and was introduced to the concept of an overlay. The way this works is that you trace your pattern onto a transparent material. When aligned with your background block, you slip the appliqué piece between the overlay and the background, lining up the edges of the template with the line on the overlay. The overlay is removed and the shape is stitched.

When ready to apply the next shape, place the overlay again and align the next shape and stitch.

There are several materials you can use for the overlay. My favorite is clear upholstery vinyl. When

I trace the pattern I use a permanent marker. The pattern will not smudge and I can clearly see where my appliqué pieces go.

There are other materials that can be used for the overlay. Some people like to use a light interfacing fabric that they stitch to one edge of the block, assuring that the overlay is placed uniformly when they add the next piece. I must admit, this is not my choice. That overlay adds more bulk to my work as I hold my background block to stitch. I constantly turn my block as I work so eventually that extra fabric of the overlay will end up in my hand. Some overlays are made from an overhead transparency plastic sheet. This works great if the design is small enough to fit on an 8 1/2" x 11" sheet of paper as it can be run through a copy machine or printer, eliminating the hand-tracing step. If the design is larger than a sheet of paper, copy or print the sections and tape them together with transparent tape.

Preparing the Background

Whatever placement technique you use, you will need to mark the center lines of the block. Begin by folding the square in half and finger press a crease. (Don't use an iron or it will be there forever!) Open the block, give it a 1/4-turn and fold again, aligning the first crease. Finger press again. This folded grid will align with the quadrant markings for all the patterns included in this book.

Appliqué Methods

Needleturn

In my opinion, needleturn appliqué is the easiest method of appliqué. In the long run, I find it to be the least preparation intensive. Once the templates are traced onto the right side of the fabric and the seam allowance is cut, you're ready to turn under the seam allowance and stitch.

My favorite template material for needleturn is freezer paper. Trace the pattern onto the paper (non-shiny) side of the freezer paper, taking care to include any symbols and the numbers, which is your stitching sequence. Because the template will go onto the right side of your fabric, you won't need to reverse the pattern first. When tracing your pattern, trace the entire line drawing as you see it, not each individual shape separately. You will want to maintain the relationship between shapes. That is, if you alter a shared line in any way, the changes will be made to both shapes equally, therefore they will fit together again perfectly.

Cut the pattern apart on the lines once the pattern is traced onto the freezer paper. I do this at the ironing board. Arrange the fabrics you plan to use in your design on the ironing board surface. As you cut the shapes apart, "deal" them to the appropriate fabrics. While cutting the freezer paper templates, remember seam allowance is in fabric,

never in the paper. Therefore, just cut on your drawn lines without adding anything extra for seam allowance. Once the templates are all cut apart, arrange them on the right side of the fabrics, leaving at least 3/4" between shapes for seam allowance, orienting them so the majority of the edges are on the bias. Bias edges make for easier turning of the seam allowances as you stitch. (I will tell you, though, there is at least one noted appliqué artist who suggests that turning the pieces on the bias instead of matching the grain of the background will cause your appliqué shapes to twist as you stitch, causing the appliqué to appear less than smooth. It is suggested, even, that one use lined paper for the template instead of freezer paper, unless preprinted with a grid, so the lines in the paper can guide placement of the template on the straight of the grain in the appliqué fabric. I still prefer freezer paper templates and bias edges. I take extra care not to twist or distort my appliqué pieces.)

Press a dry iron, set on the wool setting, onto the templates to adhere the freezer paper to the fabric. If you find the templates don't stay attached to the fabric, you may have a cool iron (some brands do seem to be cooler than others) and you will need to set the iron on the cotton setting. But start with the wool setting just in case your iron is especially hot.

Once the templates are all adhered to the fabrics, trace the templates. Because the freezer paper is easy to remove, you will need to use a slightly altered method of tracing so as not to slip

the template away from the fabric. I have found tracing over the top of the template to work the best. That is, as I am holding the marker (light for dark fabric and dark for light fabric) the template will be between my hand and the marker tip. Tracing "over the top" will not loosen the template from the fabric as tracing up against the template would. And don't forget to put that sandpaper board under the fabric as you trace.

After all the templates are traced, cut your seam allowances. You may find 1/8" to be too narrow a seam allowance, depending on the weave of your fabric. You will find 1/4" always to be too much fabric. I recommend splitting the difference and striving for a 3/16" seam allowance in most cases. However, a very small appliqué shape would obviously not benefit by a 3/16" seam allowance.

(See photo on top of page 12.)

To stitch the appliqué, place it using the overlay as a guide. Don't remove the template until after you have placed and secured the shape with a couple of pins in the seam allowance. Once you are satisfied with the placement, slip a needle or pin between the paper and the fabric to release the template without stretching the fabric. Move the pins to the interior of the shape, taking care not to shift the shape.

Where you begin stitching is important. You never want to begin at a point, inside or outside, unless that point is created by another piece overlapping the first. But if you have a point that you will turn, you must start at least 1/4″ before. If I am stitching an oval leaf with points on both ends, I will begin about 1/4″ to 1/2″ before the point that is located next to the stem on a relatively straight spot, so when I complete stitching the shape I don't have a distortion at the join. This way I have more control over the leaf's placement. If I am going to shift the leaf at all, I don't want that shift to occur at the stem. If the shape is not overlapped by another, I usually start stitching on a relatively straight side.

Choose thread to match the appliqué fabric. Begin by knotting the thread (the end you cut from the spool if the thread is made in Europe or Japan, the leading end if made in the United States) with a "quilter's knot." (If you are left handed, make your knot on the leading end if you are using European or Japanese thread and the cut end if American made.) Bring the needle up from the reverse side of the appliqué fabric on the traced line, thus placing the knot in the fold of the appliqué and not on the reverse side of the block. With the tip of the needle, prick the seam allowance and then with the shaft of the needle, drag the seam allowance under until the traced line disappears. Take a small stitch into the background just under the fold right where the thread is coming out of the fold, then come up through the appliqué and out in the edge of the fold. All of your forward progression will be on the back side of the block. The next stitch is again right where

the thread comes out of the fold, in the background just under the edge of the fold. If you are left handed, stitch clock-wise around the shape – from left to right. If you are right handed, stitch counter clock-wise around the shape – from right to left.

If you can see your stitches, one of two things may be happening. If you see little "thorns" around your appliqué edge, you are beginning your stitch in the background next to the folded edge instead of just under the edge of the fold. If you see your stitches on the edge of the appliqué, your needle is coming up through the top of the appliqué instead of out of the fold and wrapping the edge of the appliqué. If the edge of your appliqué has a "scalloped" appearance, you are probably pulling your thread too tightly.

To avoid thread tails that can shadow through your finished quilt, don't tie knots to end. I take my last stitch, and then I take another stitch just like it in the same place and in the opposite direction. Then I take that last stitch again which, in essence, creates a figure 8, locking the thread. My last task is to place the needle into the hole the thread is coming from, travel an inch or so in the fold of the appliqué, taking care not to penetrate the background, bring the needle out of the top and clip the thread right at the surface of the fabric, leaving the tail in the fold of the appliqué.

I believe how you hold your block while you stitch and how you position the needle are very important to your stitching health. Keeping your wrists relaxed and straight will help prevent hand problems such as Carpal Tunnel Syndrome.

Stitch with your thumb at right angle to the edge of the appliqué. Stitching with your thumb parallel to the edge causes you to bend your wrist sharply. Hold the needle so that it is parallel to the appliqué edge. Angling it in toward the turned under edge will not let you use the length of the needle to turn under the seam allowance. In fact, by keeping your wrists relaxed and straight, you will notice that your thumb and the needle form a "T."

❧ Back Basting

Basting the appliqué fabric to the block from the reverse side of the block eliminates the template totally. (You pay for both sides of the fabric, so can the reverse side really be called "wrong?") This method is especially good for simple or primitive designs. However, it works for a more complicated design, too.

Begin by placing the background block, right side down, on the pattern that has been placed on a light box. Trace the pattern onto the block, using a marker that will show. I recommend using a fine line and a light hand. While the mark is indeed on the reverse side, a dark, heavy mark may shadow through and you won't want that.

Beginning with the piece numbered #1, place a piece of fabric, reverse side of appliqué fabric to right side of background block, over the appliqué shape drawn on the back. Use a piece that is at least 1/2" larger all around to accommodate any variance in the size. Using a larger shafted needle and thicker thread, stitch a small running stitch directly over the traced line. You don't have to match the thread color. In fact, a contrasting thread would be desirable. Remember, you're stitching from the back through both layers of fabric. When you turn the block over you will see an exact duplicate of the traced shape. Now trim the excess appliqué fabric, leaving a 3/16" seam allowance.

When you are ready to begin stitching, remove a short length of the basting stitches. The holes that the basting thread created in the background and in the appliqué will be your stitching guide. Needleturn the seam allowance so the fold is matching the basting holes in the appliqué and meets the basting holes in the background. Stitch the appliqué with the same techniques described on page 12, using matching thread. Do not turn under the edge that will be covered by another appliqué shape in the stitching sequence. Remove the basting stitches as

you work. The basting will keep your appliqué shape in place and the basting holes will not disappear before you finish.

When you turn the block over, you will notice your stitching will be directly over the traced lines. If they don't match exactly, however, no one will know!

⇶ Mylar Template and Starch

If you find turning under the seam allowance as you stitch to be too cumbersome, there are a variety of techniques that you can use to prepare the appliqué, securing the seam allowance before you stitch.

Begin by gathering appliqué fabric, a sheet of Mylar template plastic, available at your local quilt shop, liquid starch, a small paint brush, your iron and ironing surface. Trace the pattern onto the Mylar template plastic with a permanent marker, taking care to add the stitch sequence numbering.

Cut the templates out. This time you will be working from the reverse side of the fabric, so you will be placing the right side of the template against the reverse side of the appliqué fabric. You will want to make sure you don't reverse that or you will end up with a mirror image of the design, or if you're not consistent you will notice some pieces won't fit. Cut a seam allowance around the shape, taking care not to be too skimpy.

Place the appliqué fabric, right side down on the ironing surface, and center the template, right side of template against reverse side of fabric. Place a small amount of the liquid starch in a dish or spray some into the lid, and dip the paint brush into the starch. Paint the seam allowance with the starch.

Using the brush as a tool, wrap the seam allowance around the template a little at a time and press with the hot iron to dry the starch, securing the seam allowance. You will have to clip inside curves and inside points. The appliqué edges should be smooth, with no pleats. Do not turn the seam allowance if it will be overlapped by a subsequent shape.

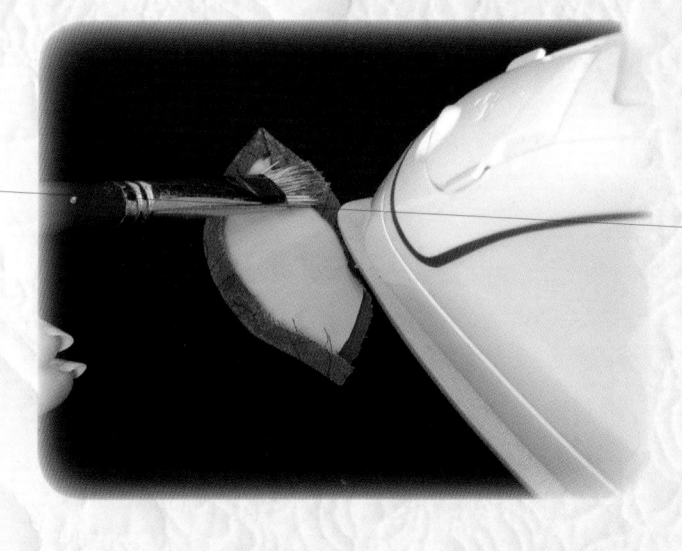

When you are ready to stitch, carefully loosen the seam allowance from the template and slip the template out from under the seam allowance. Take care to disturb the seam allowance as little as possible. Stitch the appliqué using the same technique as described on page 12.

You can accomplish the same technique with freezer paper as you can with the Mylar Template Plastic as described previously. I did this by tracing the pattern on the non-shiny side of a sheet of freezer paper. I then ironed a second sheet over the first, making a stiffer template. Following the same steps as described above, I prepared my appliqué shapes.

I have even heard of some people making their templates from cardboard such as used in cereal boxes or that which come in new men's shirts or even file folders. They then place a piece of appliqué fabric, right side down on a piece of aluminum foil and sprayed with starch. The template is then centered over that. The aluminum foil is wrapped around the template, pulling the fabric seam allowance over the template. When a hot iron is touched to the shape, the starch is evaporated, the edge is creased and the aluminum foil holds the package all together.

This seems like a lot of work to me and I don't think I would have the control over the edges that I desire. So you will not find me employing this technique in my appliqué work. But if it works for you, GREAT! My goal here is to provide you with enough information that you can find what works best for you so you will enjoy appliqué as much as I do.

❧ Basted Freezer Paper

Begin by reversing the pattern so as to make a mirror imaged pattern. Trace the pattern onto the paper (non-shiny) side of a sheet of freezer paper. Cut the templates apart and iron each one to the reverse side of the appliqué fabric. Trim the excess to a 3/16" seam allowance.

Turn under the seam allowance and with needle and thread-baste it in place. Take care that your edges stay smooth. Do not turn under any edge that will be covered by a subsequent shape. Stitch using the same techniques described on page 10.

When the appliqué is complete, remove the basting stitches. On the back of the block, cut the background out from behind the appliqué and gently remove the freezer paper.

You can accomplish the same technique without thread-basting the seam allowance if you use a washable glue stick on the reverse side of the seam allowance. When you turn under the seam allowance, it will adhere to the freezer paper and stay in place as you appliqué. When all the appliqué is complete, you will have to wet the block to loosen the glue. Again, cut the background out from behind the appliqué and gently remove the freezer paper template.

And yet another method would be to trace the pattern onto the non-shiny side of the freezer paper without reversing the pattern first. Cut the templates out and place the template on the reverse side of the fabric — right side of template against reverse side of fabric. Turn the seam allowance to the back over the template and iron to the shiny side of the template. This will hold the seam allowance in place as you stitch — just as the basting did in the previous example.

Stitch the appliqué to your block. As with the basted method, remove the background from behind the appliqué shapes and remove the paper templates.

The Pots de Fleurs Quilt

Pots de Fleurs
89" x 89"
Made by Kathy Delaney, Overland Park, Kansas
Quilted by Kelly Ashton, Overland Park, Kansas

Pots de Fleurs

❧ Fabric Requirements

Background

(While I used the same fabric for the blocks, borders and binding, you may wish to use a variety. Therefore, I list the fabrics below separately.)

- ❀ 3 1/4 yards for blocks – (9) 22" squares [19" finished]
- ❀ 2 3/4 yards for borders – 10" finished
- ❀ 1/2 yard for inner border
- ❀ 1/2 yard for piping
- ❀ 3/4 yard for binding

Pots

- ❀ 1/3 – 1/2 yard each of 4 or 5 gradations of hand dyed blue for all of the pots in this quilt

Appliqué

Blocks

A guide for the flower appliqué fabrics for each block is listed with each block.

Border

(The hand-dyed fabrics I used are mottled. That is, there are variations in the value within each piece, while the overall shade varies from piece to piece. Therefore, some of the scrolls are darker than others; some circles are lighter than others and sometimes lighter or darker than the scrolls. The hearts are darker still.)

- ❀ 1 1/2 yards hand dyed blue #1 (over-all medium light) for scrolls
- ❀ 1/3 yard hand dyed blue #2 (over-all medium) for circles and "drops"
- ❀ 1/2 yard hand dyed blue #3 (over-all medium dark) for hearts

⁓ The Blocks

Preparing the Blocks

The blocks will finish to a 19" square block. Begin with a 22" square of background fabric. Once all the appliqué is complete you will trim the block to a 19 1/2" square.

Use your favorite method to do the appliqué. I prefer needleturn appliqué. That is, I use my needle (a #11 Straw or Milliner) to turn under my seam allowance as I stitch. I turn under about 1/4" ahead of my stitching, just what my thumbnail can hold. Any more, and I won't have a nice smooth edge to my curves. (Note – there are quilters who use Sharps or even Betweens with which to appliqué. Use what works best for you.)

I used freezer paper for my pot and flower templates unless otherwise noted. Trace the pot and each of the flowers, as a unit, on the paper side of freezer paper. You will not need a template for the free standing stems. Number the pieces as per the pattern (this is the stitching sequence). When you cut the shapes apart, notice that any changes to a shared line you make with your scissors will make equal changes to both pieces. This means the pieces will sew together perfectly. Iron the templates onto the right side of the appliqué fabric with a dry iron set on the wool setting. I try to place the template so the majority of the edges will be on the bias for easier turning. Trace around the outside of the template. As you sew, note the line is turned under,

as is the seam allowance. Before you begin, please see the directions for "piecing the appliqué," on page 21.

I used a clear upholstery vinyl on which to trace the block for a placement overlay. Be sure to include the center and side-center markings for placement purposes. Fold the background block in half, finger press, open, rotate a quarter turn and fold again, aligning the first crease and ignoring the edges, and crease. These folds will match the markings on the overlay.

Finishing the block

When you have finished stitching the appliqué, place the block, right side down, onto a clean fluffy terry towel. Press with an up and down motion, don't iron. I like steam, but others often don't — your choice. Once you have pressed the block, trim the block to measure 19 1/2" square.

Techniques Used Often

Some techniques are used repeatedly in many of the blocks and will be described here. Some techniques are used for specific blocks and will be described with the patterns.

Piecing the Appliqué – Pot and Flowers

Traditionally the appliqué shapes are stitched to the background blocks. I prefer to remove the background from behind the appliqué when possible so I can quilt by hand more successfully. If each of the shapes is stitched, one by one, to the background, I cannot remove all the layers of fabric I need to. Therefore, I study each piece and determine which part of each shape is "background" and which is the "appliqué."

The "background" is any part that will be under an adjacent shape. The "appliqué" is any part that will be stitched, that is, the seam allowance is turned under and the edge stitched to the background block or the adjacent piece. If the part of a shape is the "background," I leave about 3/4" or more so I have someplace to pin-baste the next piece while I'm stitching. On the part of the shape that is the "appliqué," I cut a 3/16" seam allowance. Please note, 1/4" is too much fabric to turn under and 1/8" is often too narrow, especially if you have

a loosely woven fabric for the appliqué, so split the difference.

As I build the unit and stitch each "appliqué," I trim the "background" out from behind the appliqué before adding the next piece. That is, I remove the extra fabric I left for my pin-basting by trimming so all the seam allowances are 3/16" when I am finished. When all the pieces to a unit are stitched together and the excess is trimmed from behind, I stitch the completed unit to the background block, having to only stitch around the outside edge of the unit. This allows me to trim the background out from behind the appliqué unit, removing the excess layer of fabric for ease of hand quilting later.

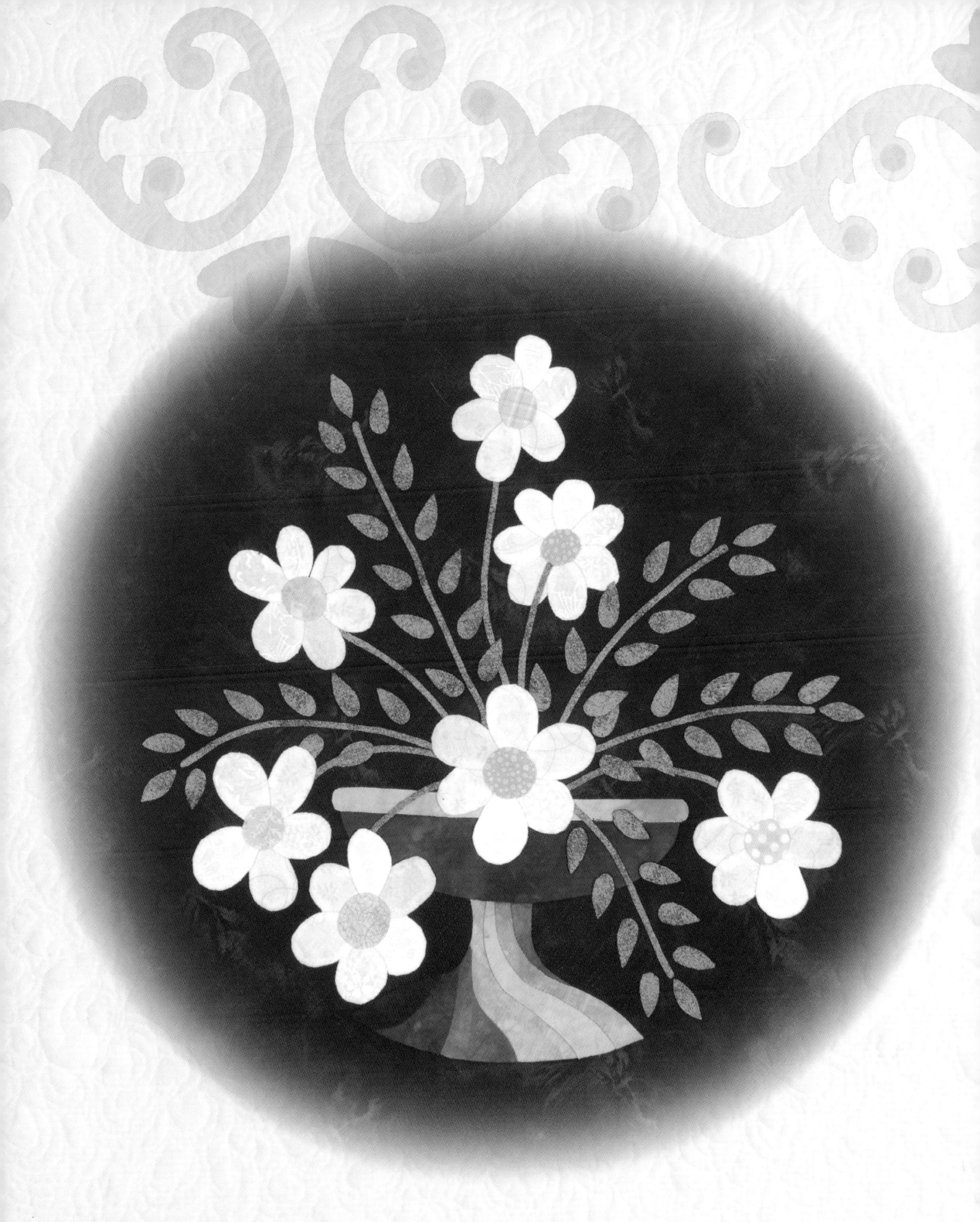

Daisies

❦ Appliqué fabric

❀ 9" x 22" green for stems and leaves

❀ (5-6) 6" squares of white and cream prints for flowers (a variety of visual texture would be good so each petal stands out separately)

❀ (5-7) 3" squares of gold for flower centers (I used different fabrics)

(Templates on begin page 77)

❦ 1/8" Stems

To make the stems on this block, I begin with 1/4" bias tape that I make using the Clover bias tape maker. I store the bias tape on an empty bathroom tissue roll or paper towel roll by rolling it on the cardboard tube and pinning to secure. Press the pin straight in through the bias tape and the tube and it will stay in place. This keeps the bias tape from developing wrinkles and it keeps the folded edges from relaxing.

To make the skinny stem, cut one of the folded sides of the bias tape on the fold. You will be left with a finished (folded) edge and a raw edge. To begin, mark your background block with a line representing the inside curve only of the stem. I mark lightly and plan to cover the mark with the bias tape. Sew the folded edge to the inside curve of the stem. Use your needle to turn the raw edge under and stitch the other side. You will have a 1/8" stem.

You can also easily make 1/8" stems free hand. Begin with a bias strip of fabric about 1" wide and about 1" longer than the stem. Fold the bias strip in half the long way, reverse side in. With a marker or a Hera Marker, make a line 1/8" from the fold. I like to use the mechanical pencil but some of my students have noted the Hera Marker works well for them. I think it works best on a fabric with little or no print.

1.

2.

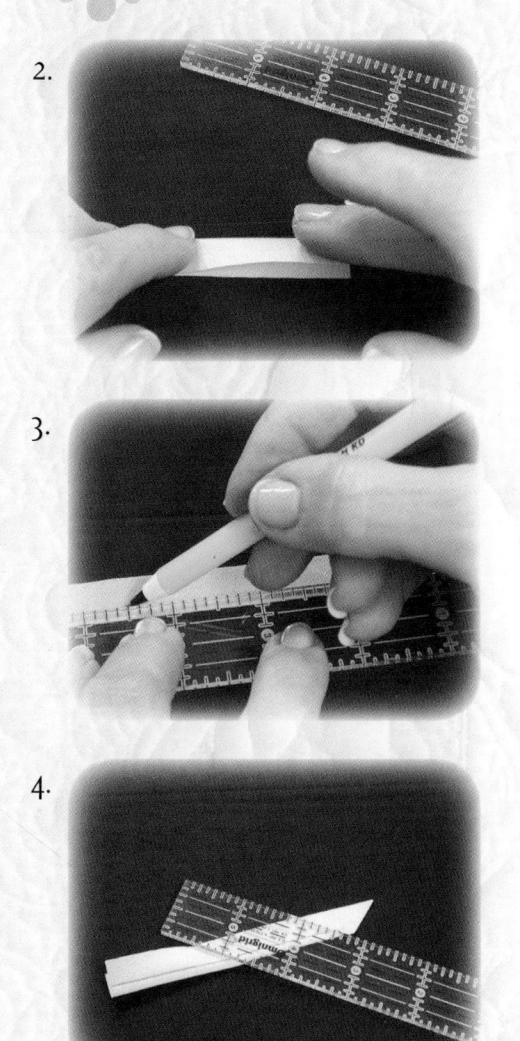

3.

4.

5.

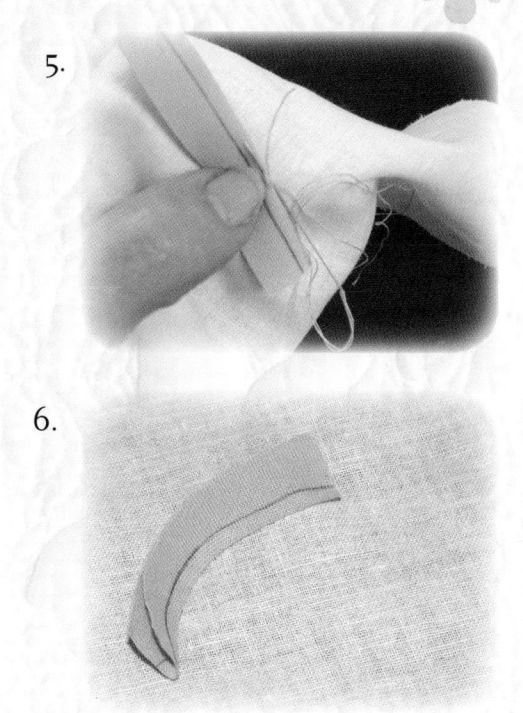

6.

Open the strip so that part is now on the inside of the circle and hold it down with your thumb. Now you are holding the appliqué from inside the circle. With your embroidery scissors that are sharp all the way to the tip, trim the excess fabric on the outside of the circle close to the stitching. You don't need that excess fabric anymore now that the edge has been stitched.

7.

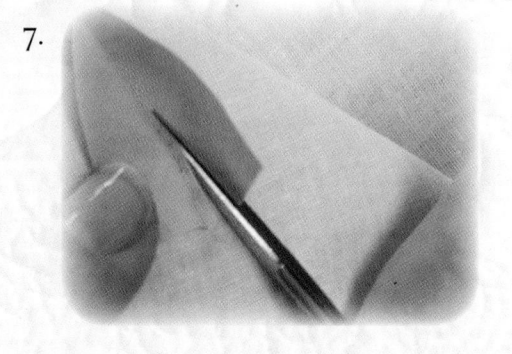

Mark the inside curve of the stem on your background as described above. It is important that you place the strip correctly. So, consider the line you drew on the background to be part of a circle. The side of the line that is inside the circle is called the inside curve. The space outside that circle would be called the outside curve. Place the fold of the bias strip on the line so that all of the excess is outside the circle. You will be holding the appliqué from the outside of the circle and will be stitching on the inside. Stitch from one end of the line to the other end of the line and stop.

8.

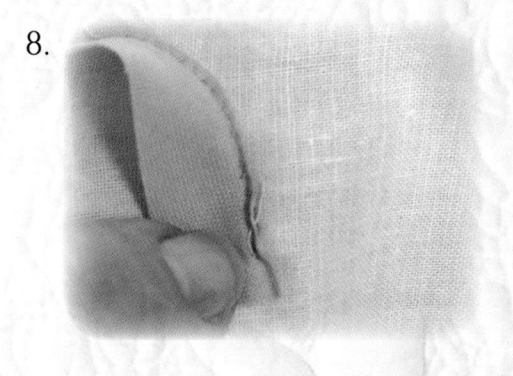

Flip the fold from inside the circle back over as it was when you appliquéd the bias strip to the circle. Trim the remaining half of the strip 1/8" from the mark you drew. Needleturn the seam allowance under and stitch, using the mark you drew as your turn under guide.

9.

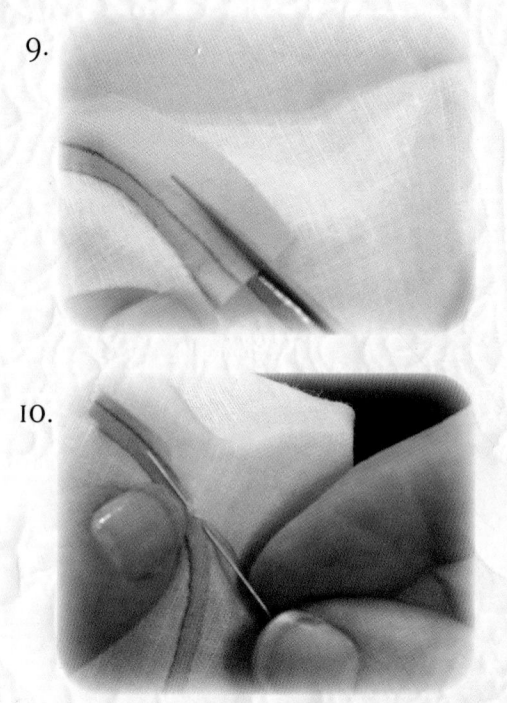

10.

✤ Leaves

All the leaves along the sides of the stems are the same size and shape. The leaves at the ends of the stems are a second shape. I used a template

plastic for my leaf template. Trace the two leaf shapes onto the template plastic. With a craft knife, carefully cut the leaf shape out, cutting just outside the line or on the outside edge of the drawn line, leaving the background to the shape intact. You will use this "window" to trace the shape directly onto the right side of the leaf fabric. By cutting the window slightly larger, you will be compensating for the fact that the traced line is turned under when you stitch. Otherwise, your leaves will be smaller than the ones drawn in the pattern.

I recommend using a mechanical pencil, such as the Clover Mechanical Pencil or the Bohin Mechanical Pencil, for marking the turn-under lines. The lead maintains an even, fine line so your leaves will not be distorted. Both of the marker leads come in a variety of colors: white, gray/silver, yellow and pink and green. I find the gray works for me for everything, from light to dark, but medium blue or gray. I cut a very narrow seam allowance, about 1/8", since the leaves are so small.

Dimensional tip: Just before adding your final stitches to the Daisy center, add a little Fiberfil to give the flower a puffy look. You could stuff the petals, as well, for more dimension.

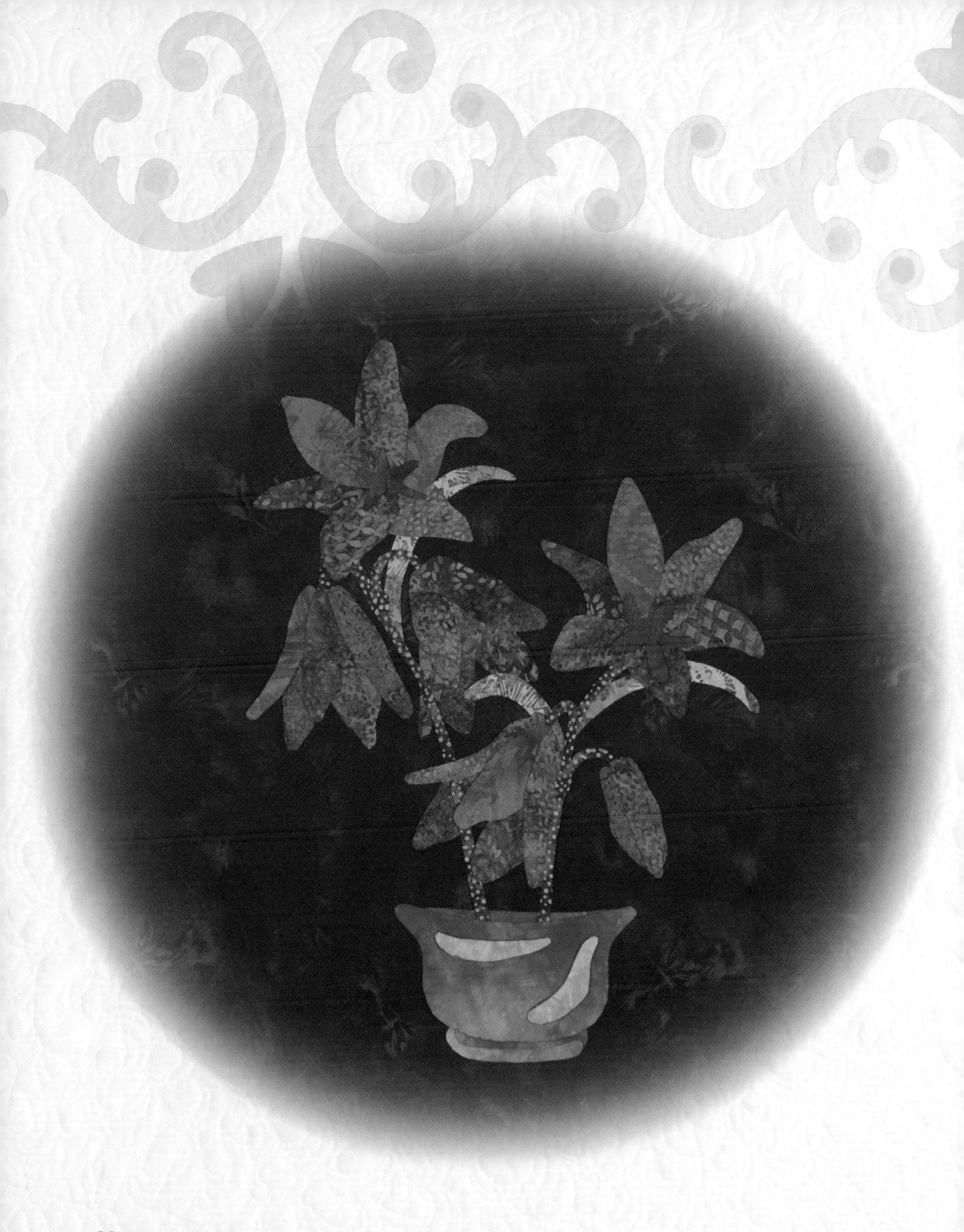

Chocolate Lily

⇛ Appliqué fabric

❀ 7" x 10" green for stems

❀ 5" x 6" green for leaves

❀ 6" x 10" each of 5 rust prints (bright to dark)
for flower petals

❀ 3" x 5" purple for flower centers

(Templates begin on page 81)

While teaching in Alaska, a student gave me a
wonderful gift. It was a coloring book full of Alaskan
wild flowers. After the intensity of the Siberian
Poppy, I needed a break! So I chose this very simple
flower from the coloring book for this block.

These lilies provided quite a design challenge
for me, however. The actual flower is centered with
a cluster of stamens. I took artistic license and
changed them to the star shape so as to be easier
to stitch. I found it quite easy to piece the appliqué
where these flowers are concerned. All in all, these
flowers were quite a bit simpler than some of the
previous flowers!

I used the Cut Away method to stitch the stems.
Refer to page 47 for a review of this technique.

⇛ The Pot

This pot represents a silver Revere bowl. I
appliquéd the highlights onto the tracing of the pot
first. Once the highlight appliqué was finished on the
pot, I cut the seam allowance for the pot. This way
I didn't have frayed seam allowances to stitch to the
block background.

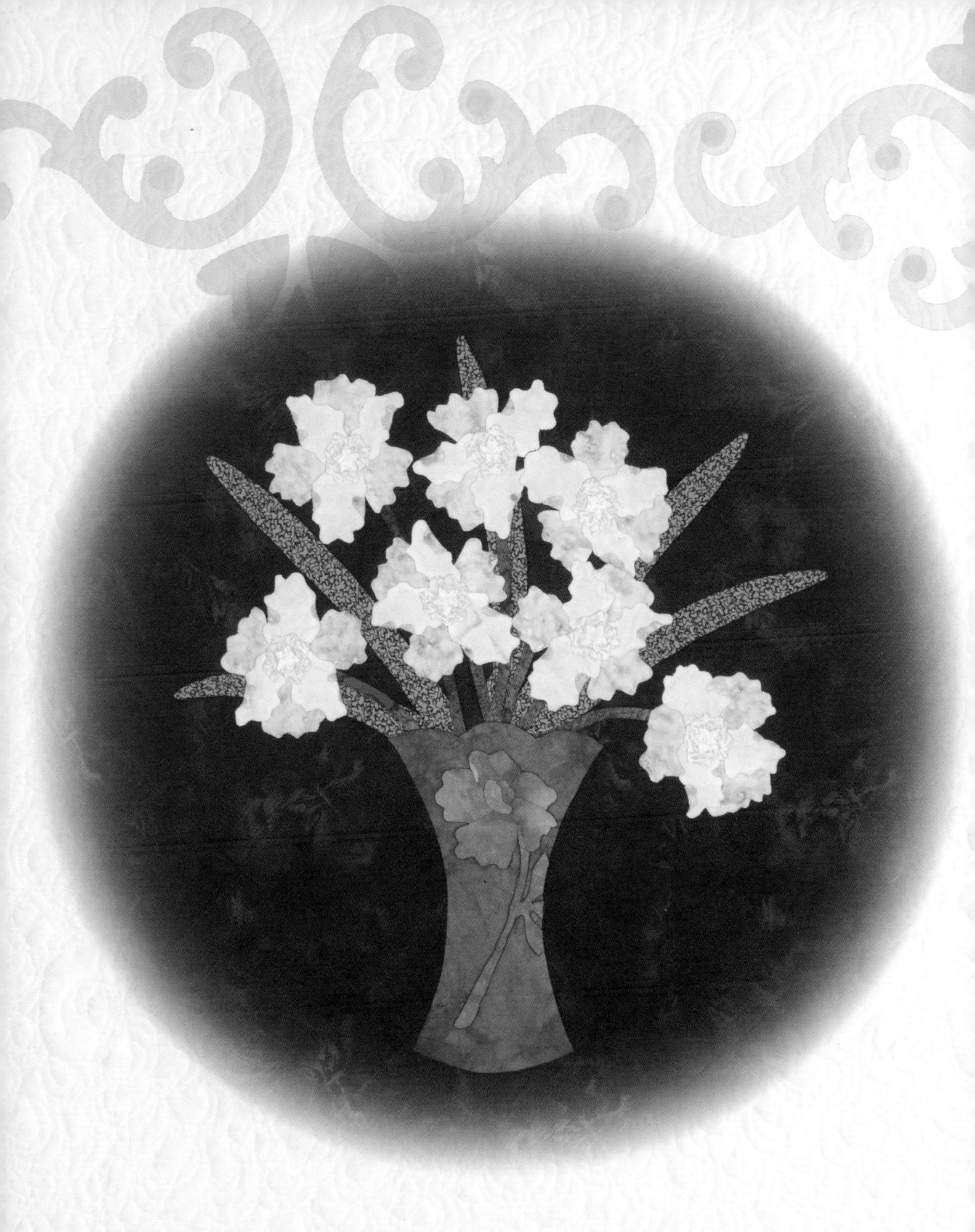

Siberian Poppy

❧ Appliqué fabric

🌸 8" x 10" green for leaves

🌸 8" x 10" dark green for bias stems

🌸 12" x 14" light blue for petals

🌸 12" x 14" medium blue for petals

🌸 4" x 7" medium yellow for flower centers

🌸 3" x 4" light yellow for flower centers

(Templates begin on page 85)

❧ Curly Edges

The petals of these poppies are designed to appear very lacy on the edges — very curly. Originally I had planned the petals to be appliquéd to the tiny pieces on the edges that represent the underside of the petals. I thought it might be easier to sew. However, I changed my mind as I wanted those tiny pieces to appear to be on top of the petal, which would have been more natural and because they represent a curling edge. I've numbered the pattern to reflect this, but feel free to stitch it the way that would be most comfortable to you.

Even though the pieces are smaller, they are stitched the same way a larger flower would be stitched — one stitch at a time.

I created the stems by making 1/4-inch bias tape.

❧ Adding dimension

Notice this block on Mindy's quilt on page 76. Mindy actually faced each of the petals. That is, she cut the petals from two fabrics, sewed the right sides together at the ends and turned. Depending on how deeply you turn back the edges of the petals, you may get away with sewing half the reverse petal to the back of each petal. When appliquéing the petals to the background, turn back the tips to expose the finished back side. This will accomplish the same look as I did with my appliqué.

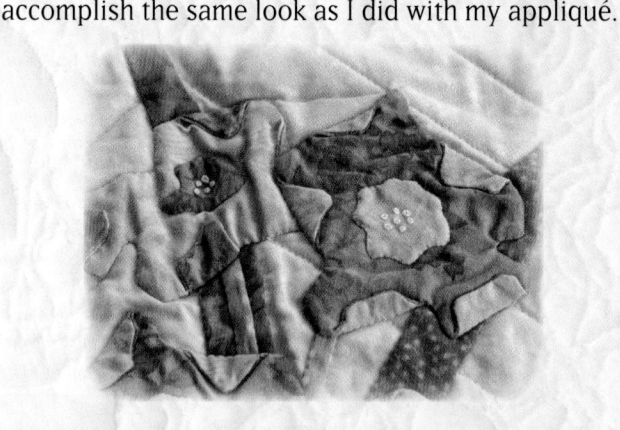

❧ The Pot

I pieced the appliqué flower that decorates the pot first and then stitched it to the pot shape. I cut the seam allowance for the stem as I stitched — just like the rose block.

Once the appliqué was finished on the pot, I cut the seam allowance for the pot. This way I didn't have distortion or frayed seam allowances to stitch to the block background.

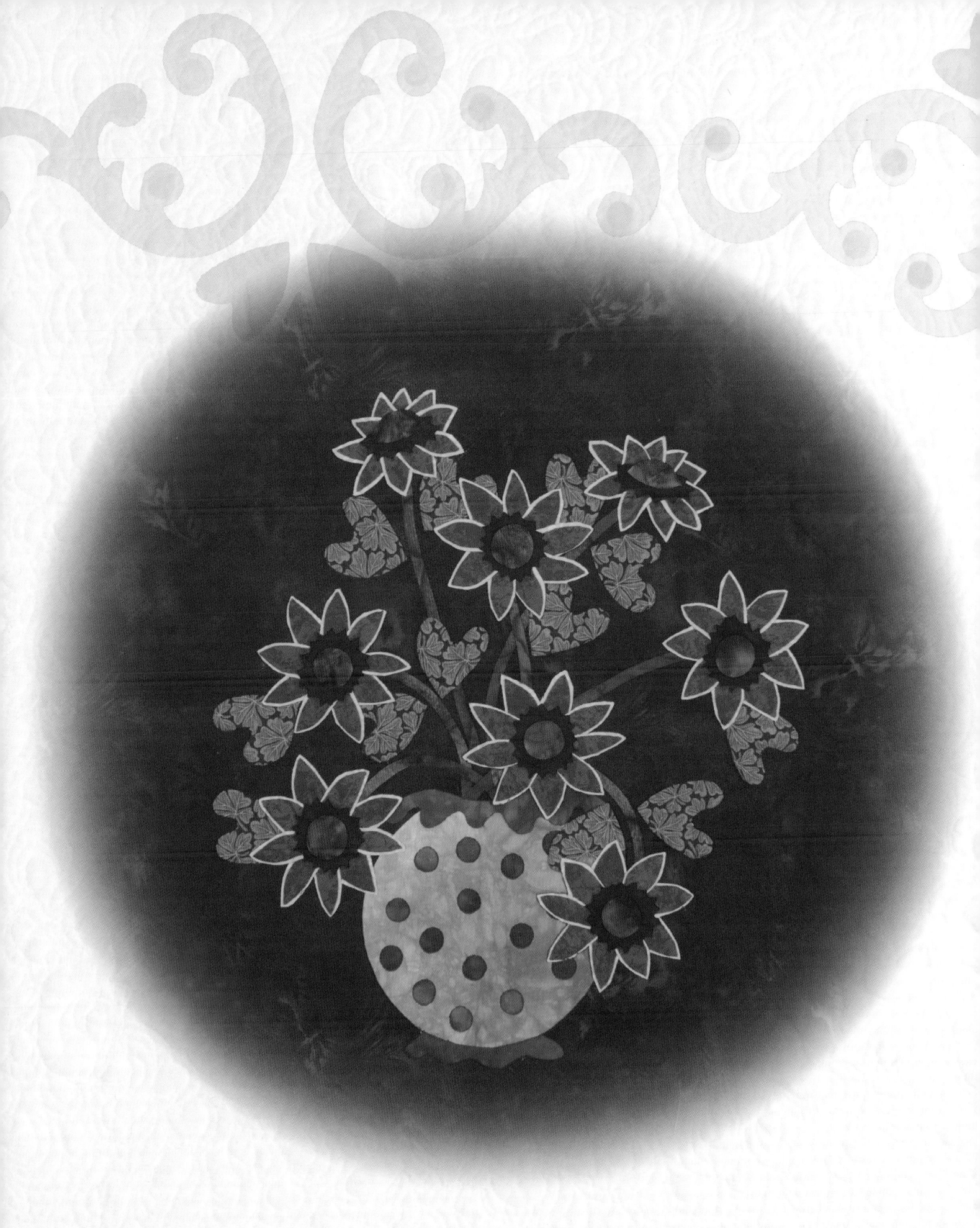

Black-Eyed Susan

🍃 Appliqué fabric

🌸 9" x 15" orange for petals

🌸 12" x 22" yellow for petals

🌸 8" x 10 1/2" green for leaves

🌸 8" x 7" medium-dark green for bias stems

🌸 3" x 6" brown for flower center

🌸 6" x 10 1/2" black for flower center

(Templates begin on page 89)

🍃 Outlining appliqué

The yellow edges to the petals are accomplished very similarly to the Tulips in the Tulip block. I did not trace the base of the petal center, however. It occurred to me it would be much easier to get the center ring placed if I didn't have to try to align the edges with marks. No traced lines means no lines to cover! Just remember to leave extra fabric at the base of the petals so you have something to hold while stitching the center ring. Trim the seam allowance after stitching. (Refer to "piecing the appliqué" on page 21.)

Trace the flowers onto the non-shiny side of the freezer paper but when tracing the petals, only trace the side edges of the inner petal. You really don't need a template for the outer edge of the petals.

Begin by stitching the petals to a 12" x 22" piece of the bright yellow. I stitched all the petals to this piece before cutting seam allowance in the yellow. Just be sure to leave enough space between the orange pieces to accommodate seam allowance in the yellow – about 1/2". You need not bother trimming the yellow out from behind the orange. There wasn't enough to worry about and it gave the flowers some dimension. I marked the long sides of the petals on the orange fabric but made no marks on the yellow.

When constructing the flowers and stitching to the background I just turned the yellow under until there was just a sliver of yellow. I also attempted to alter the width of the slivers to look more natural. This sounds so much more complicated than it is but really turned out to be easy.

You will notice I did not number the yellow petal edges on the pattern. Once you have stitched all the petals to the yellow and cut the new seam allowance, treat them as one with the same numbering as before you added the yellow edge. When I completed stitching an orange petal to the yellow, I put the template back onto the orange petal and tacked it in place with two or three stitches. This way I could keep the pieces numbered so when I put the flowers together, I would know

which petals went where. Likewise, when the flower head was complete, I pinned the numbered "collar" template to the center so I knew which flower went where as I stitched the flowers to the background block.

 Circles

There are a variety of methods for making circles. Some quilters make a standard yo-yo and stitch it to the background. You may stitch the yo-yo with the gathered side down for a "stuffed" look or up for a textured look. Take a look at Mindy's quilt on page 71. She eliminated the "collar" around the center and used the yo-yo for dimension.

Some quilters will use starch to aid in making a crisp edge to the circle. I'll admit, I don't do that but you certainly may! I used the 7/8" Mylar washers from the hardware store, which work much better than a metal washer or coin as they are very thin, affording my circle a very crisp edge. You may find sets of the washers at your local quilt shop. They are on a ring with 4 washers each of a variety of sizes. These are a very convenient product! I like to have a washer for each circle I'll be stitching so I can prepare them all at once so I usually need more than the 4 in the set. I use empty pin boxes to store my prepared circles. (My local quilt shop is happy to save them for me when they put new pins on the magnetic pin holder. You might ask someone at your shop to save the pin boxes for you, too!) If you have trouble finding the mylar washers at your local hardware store or quilt shop, you can always cut your own using a medium grit sandpaper. More important than the grit is the card stock from which the sandpaper is made. Too flimsy a paper will not stand up to the gathering process.

Begin with a square of fabric about 1 1/4" larger than your washer. I trace the washer on the reverse side of the fabric lightly just to guide me in where to stitch. Use a heavy thread, such as quilting thread, to sew a running stitch about 1/8" from the outside of the circle. Stitch too close and you won't be able to cover the washer. Stitch too far away and you will end up with pleats on the edge of your circle. Stitch that running stitch so you alternate short and long stitches. The thread for the short stitch should be on the right side of the fabric. This will ensure the gathering is held within the thread and this makes for a better yo-yo, too, when you are making them.

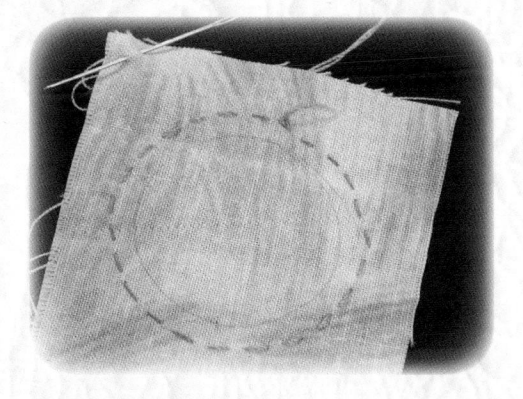

With your last stitch around the traced circle, pull the needle through to the right side, taking care you don't catch the thread of the previous stitches. Without cutting your thread, trim the excess fabric around the circle, leaving about 1/4" seam allowance outside the stitching. Return the washer to the center of the fabric, within the traced line.

Draw the thread up tight, pulling across the washer, not away from it. Rearrange the pleats so the edge is very smooth and then knot the thread to secure. Press with a hot steam iron and then hit with a clean, smooth block of wood. Hold for a few

seconds. Turn it over and repeat. The block of wood, or a klapper tool (sometimes called a "banger tool") if you have one from your tailoring days, will absorb the heat and steam and set the crease. Set the circles aside for a little while before removing the washer of one to stitch to your block, letting it dry thoroughly. Leave the other washers in place until you are ready to stitch.

To remove the washer, cut the excess fabric from the back, to about 1/8" from the edge. This will remove the excess bulk and release the stitching. Gently pull the washer out disturbing the fabric as little as possible. Be sure to save those washers for your next project!

❧ Dimensional Tip

Take a look at Mindy's quilt on page 71. Instead of making the flowers as they appear in the pattern, Mindy made yo-yos to replace the center of the flower. She actually used a tool made in Japan that makes perfect yo-yos every time. Mindy saved time and added visual interest to her flowers with the yo-yos, smooth side against the quilt.

❧ The Pot

Think traditional milk glass for this pot! The blue dots in the pot are done in reverse appliqué. Trace the dots directly onto the right side of the pot fabric. I used a circle template. You can get one at your local office supply store in the drafting department. Choose a template for a circle slightly smaller than the design circles for reverse appliqué. This will allow for the traced line. Remember, the line is part of the seam allowance so your tracing needs to be smaller to accommodate the thickness of your line.

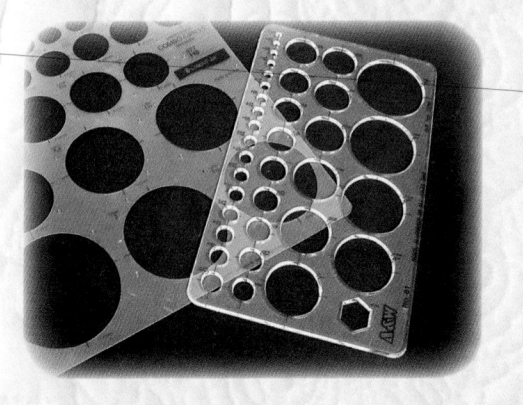

Place the dot fabric behind the pot fabric so the right side of the dot fabric is against the reverse side of the pot fabric. Open the hole, clip to the seam line and turn under the circle seam, revealing the dot fabric behind. Stitching the circles in this manner will be much easier than appliquéing these circles on top.

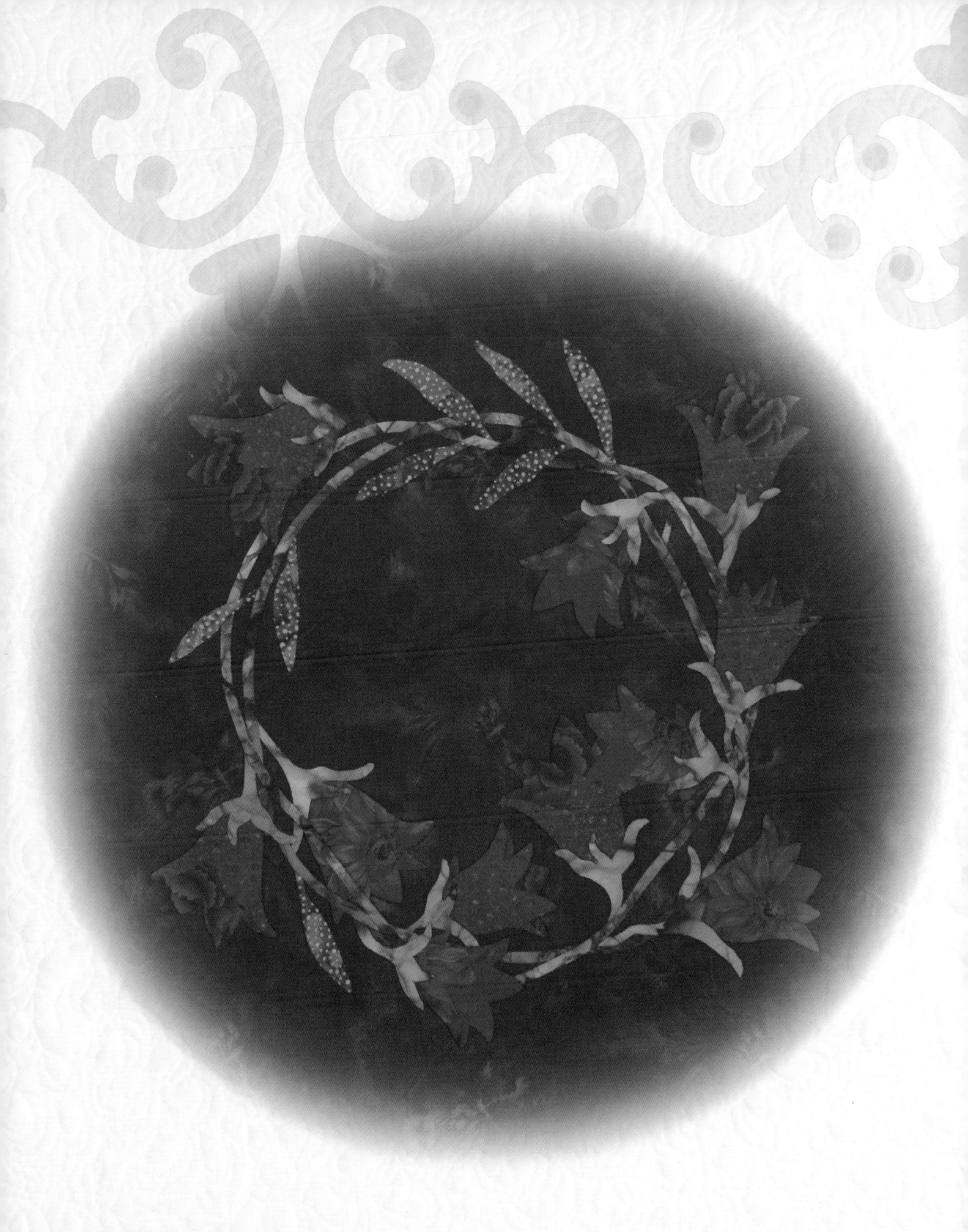

Alaskan Mountain Harebell
(my way)

❧ Appliqué fabric

❀ 9" x 22" green for stems

❀ 6" x 10" green for leaves

❀ 10" x 11" green for calyxes

❀ 8" x 10" red #1 medium for flower petals

❀ 8" x 10" red #1 dark for flower petals

❀ 8" x 10" red #2 medium for flower petals

❀ 8" x 10" red #2 dark for flower petals

(Templates begin on page 93)

❧ The Flowers

The Mountain Harebell is actually a blue flower, but I decided the quilt had enough blue and not enough red. So I took artistic license and made the flowers red. I hope you like the choice. But if you don't, remember, you can take artistic license, too!

As you stitch, take careful note of the places on the pattern that are marked "leave open." These denote places that, as you are stitching, you will want to skip and come back to stitch later. You have to do this because sometimes a piece in the design will be both over another shape and under one. The only logical way to handle them is to stitch parts of the seam allowance under, leaving a spot open to tuck in the next piece. You can stitch those spots closed as you go if you forget, but you will have to open them again when adding the next piece. Be sure to double check all the "leave open" spots before you sandwich your quilt for quilting, however. It's a lot harder to appliqué later!

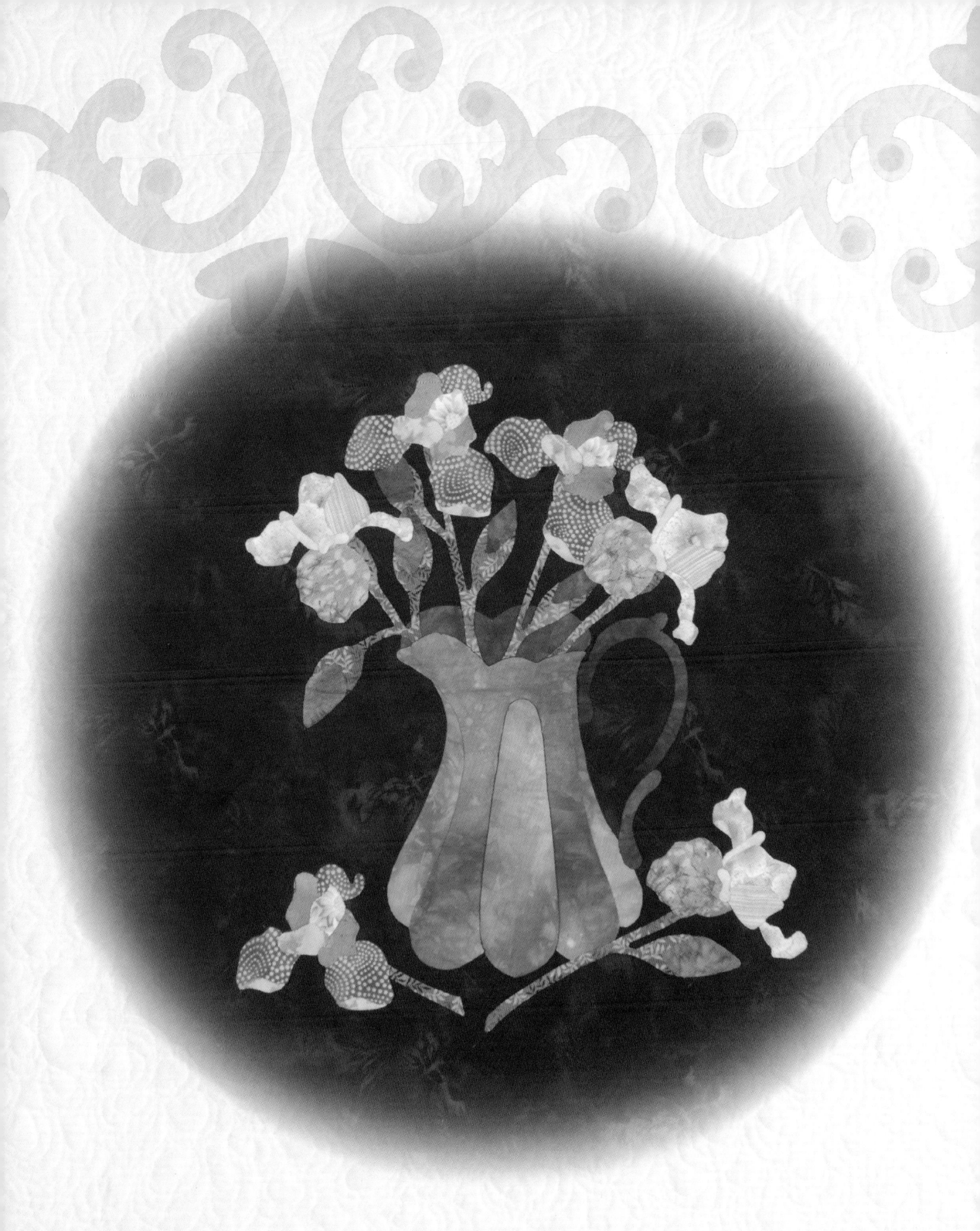

Iris

⁓ Appliqué fabric

- ✿ 3" x 4" dark purple for buds
- ✿ 5" x 10" med dark purple for petals
- ✿ 4" x 5" med purple for petals
- ✿ 5" x 5" med light purple for petals
- ✿ 2" x 4" light purple for petals
- ✿ 4" x 4" dark rose for buds
- ✿ 3" x 9" med dark rose for petals
- ✿ 6" x 6" med rose for petals
- ✿ 3" x 5" med light rose for petals
- ✿ 3" x 4" light rose for petals
- ✿ 6" x 15" green for stems

(Templates begin on page 97)

I stitched the buds to the stems before cutting any seam allowances for the stems. When stitching the stems to the background, I cut my seam allowance as I stitched, leaving me a place for my pins when I basted the shape to the background. This is the same method you use in the rose block — cut away appliqué.

Please note the very small center shape for the flower centers in the rose colored flowers. I found that I could only piece the top half of the unit and stitch it to the background. Then I added the large petal to the background. That tiny piece was added

last. Trying to piece the whole unit first would have been too difficult for me. The purple flowers were not a problem to piece first before adding to my background. (I took extra care to ensure I was being accurate in my placement and stitching. Otherwise that small piece would not have fit the center.)

You will notice there are "twisted" seams on some of the Iris flowers — on my quilt, they are in the purple flowers. You will stitch these exactly as in the leaves on the tulip block (p. 40). I stitched these in two different sequences. Follow the numbering as presented in the pattern and I think you'll find these flowers to be relatively simple. Even though the pieces are smaller, they are stitched the same way a larger flower would be stitched — one stitch at a time.

⁓ The Pot

Trace the shape #1 as one piece instead of several, even though the stems segment it. You will stitch the stems over this piece. Believe me, it will be a lot easier in the long run.

You'll notice the center of the pot is mainly two pieces, #45 and #46. I did not trace the inside line on the larger piece, #45. I thought it was easier to just place the #46 accurately and then use the traced lines on that piece for guidance to stitch the center shape. This way I didn't have to work so hard to hide both sets of lines.

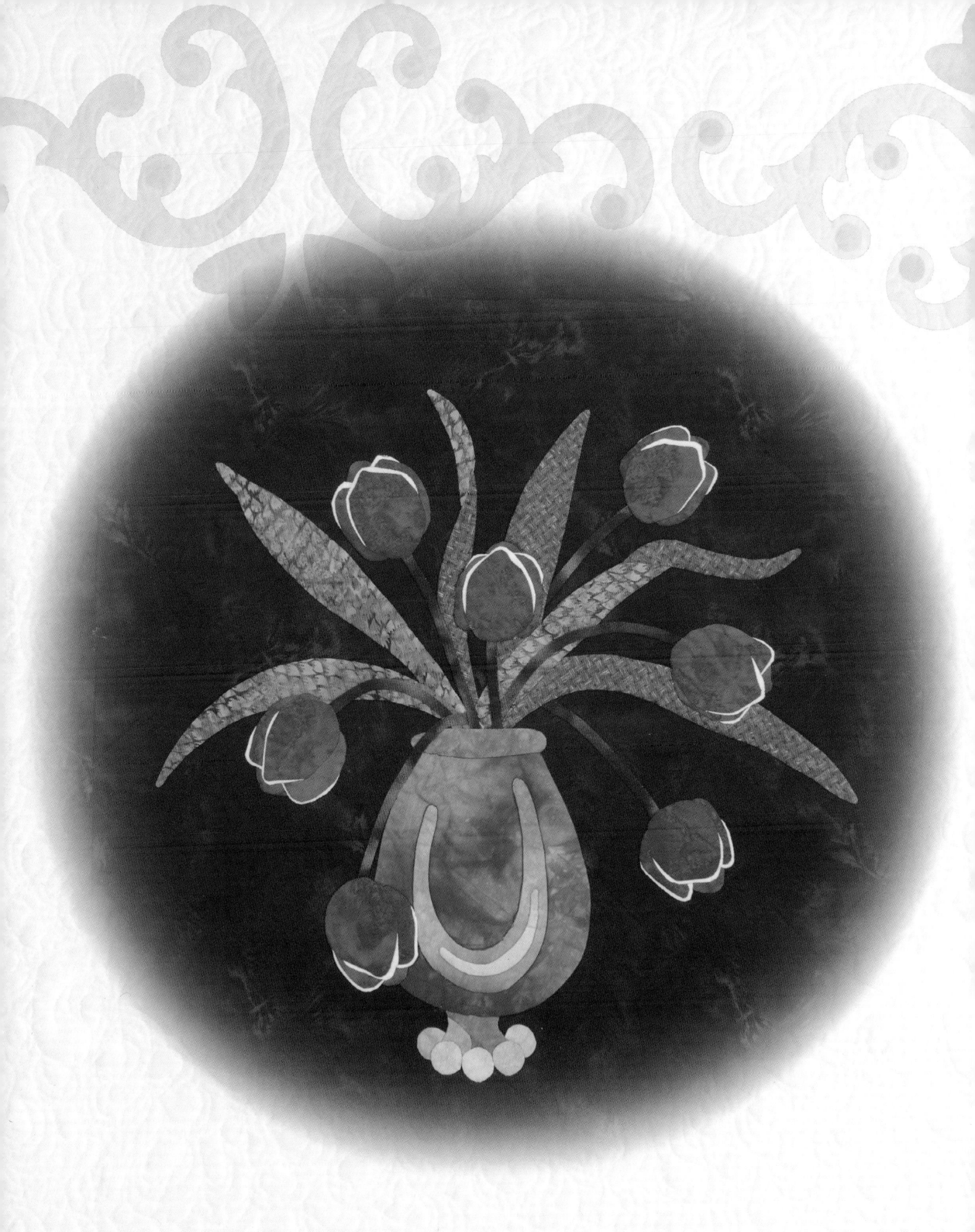

Tipped Tulips

❧ *Appliqué fabric*

✿ 10 1/2" x 18" pink for tulips

✿ 4 1/2" x 22" white for tulips

✿ 8" x 10 1/2" medium light green for leaves

✿ 7" x 15" medium green for leaves

✿ 7" x 10 1/2" medium dark green for stems

(Templates begin on page 101)

❧ *Outlining with a Sliver*

The white tips to the petals look a whole lot harder than they are! Trust me! The white tips will seem to be stitched free hand. But since there are lines traced onto the pink fabric, the appliqué shapes are very much controlled.

Trace the flowers onto the non-shiny side of the freezer paper. Before cutting the freezer paper templates apart, make a mark at the points where the pink will match the pink at the tip of the white and then be sure to transfer this mark into the seam allowances. (I just made a little mark across the junction of all the lines that met so when I cut the pieces apart each of the pieces had a matching mark.) This made fitting the pieces back together again easy since I did not use a template for the white accent in the tulip. This also told me where to start and stop stitching the pink to the white.

Begin by stitching the petal to a piece of the white. Then trim the excess from behind the petal, leaving a 3/16" seam allowance and trim the seam allowance to be turned under. About 1/4" will give you enough. I marked the pink fabric but made no marks on the white. I used a pin to match the points of connection by poking the pin straight into the layers. This let me be sure the alignment was correct before securing with another pin.

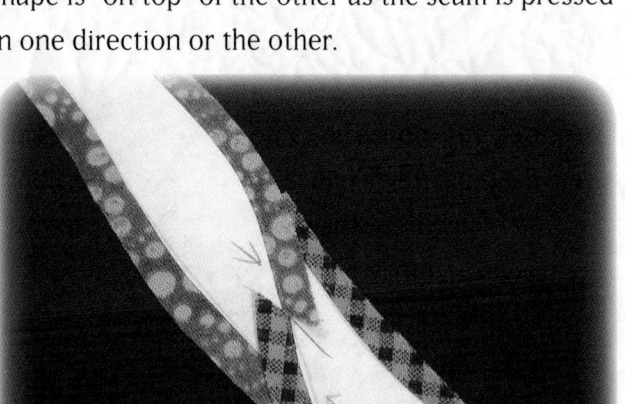

❧ Leaf Units –
twisting the seam allowance

The twisted leaves add interest to your appliqué by giving it dimension. In order to avoid having to turn a very sharp corner to create the points on these twisted leaves, I split the seam allowance so part of it can be pressed toward one direction while the other part of the same seam allowance is pressed toward the other direction. The pattern will indicate where this twist occurs by the slash mark across the seam line. The arrows indicate which shape is "on top" of the other as the seam is pressed in one direction or the other.

I just turned the white under until there was just a sliver of white showing and the folded edge matched the line of the pink shape to which this was stitched. Again, I also attempted to alter the width of the slivers to look more natural. This sounds so much more complicated than it is. Just remember, you are stitching in the same order as if you were stitching to the background block instead of piecing the appliqué. You are stitching a piece with a larger number to a piece with a smaller number. The piece with the smaller number acts as the background to the piece with the larger number. (Refer to page 21 for the instructions for "piecing the appliqué."

Without removing the template, clip the seam allowances at the slash mark, clipping just to the template. Slip the two pieces together at the clips, making sure the arrows are "on top." Turn back the templates to make stitching a little easier but don't remove the templates completely. Begin stitching from the center at the slash and stitch out to the edge. Tie off or travel back to the center through the fold and stitch out to the opposite edge. If you are careful to turn the seam allowance under so the lines are completely hidden in the seam allowance, you will not be able to see the center join at all.

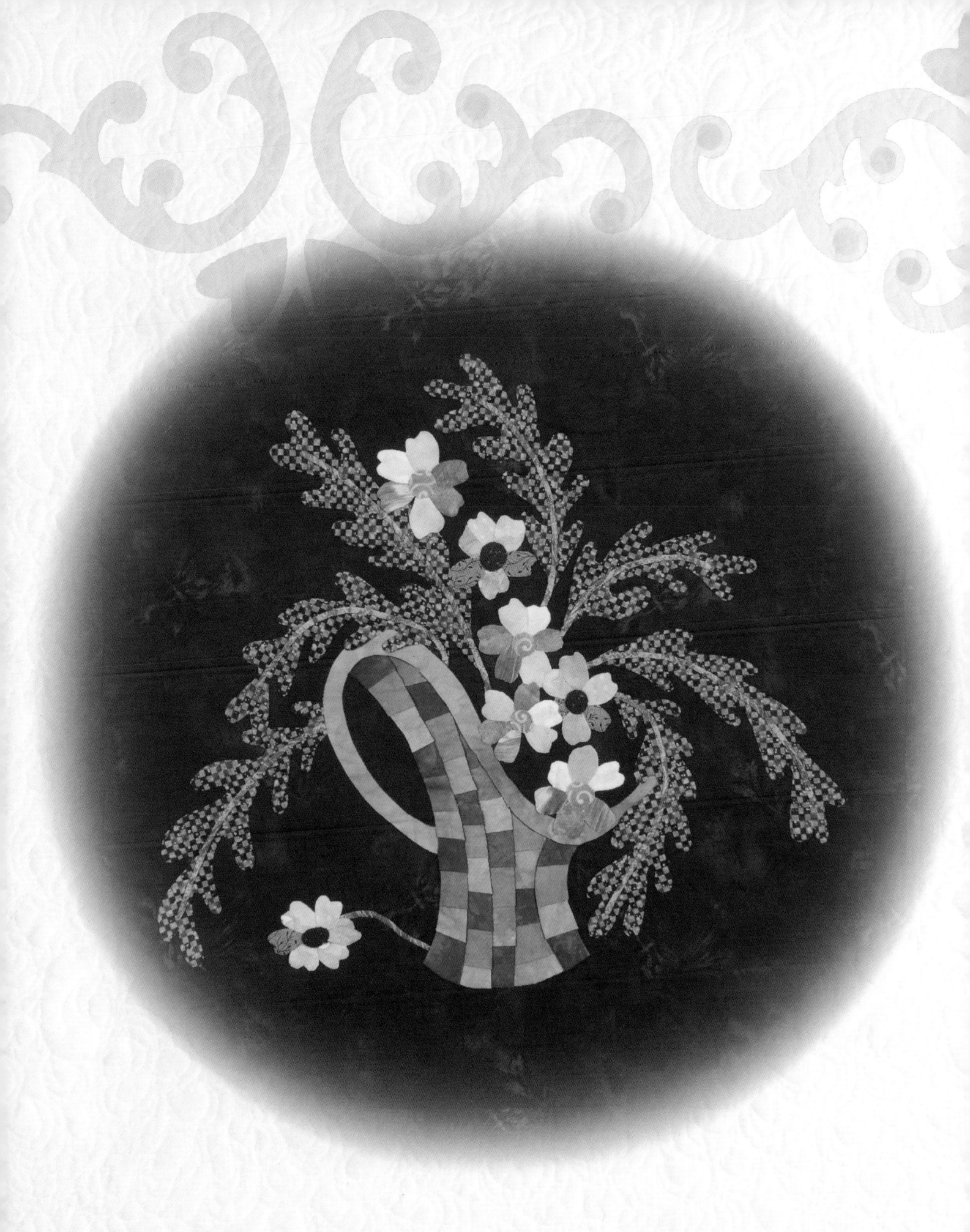

Don't Forget Me Poppy

❧ Appliqué fabric

❀ 9" x 22" green for leaves

❀ 9" x 11" green for stems

❀ (5) 5" squares of pink or peach prints for flowers (a variety of visual texture would be good so each petal stands out separately)

❀ (5) 5" squares of lavender prints for flowers (a variety of visual texture would be good so each petal stands out separately)

❀ (1) 4" square gold print for flower centers

❀ (1) 4" square deep red print for flower centers

(Templates begin on page 105)

❧ Paper Foundation with Freezer Paper

Begin by tracing the foundation pattern for the basket onto the paper side of a square of freezer paper. Notice the basket consists of vertical strips of small "squares" to form the weaving. Carefully cut the strips apart to be stitched. Notice, too, that each of the patches are marked L for light, M for medium and D for dark. Choose your fabric patches accordingly.

Cut (12) 1 1/2" squares from the light blue hand-dyed fabric. Cut (13) 1 1/2" squares from one of the medium hand-dyed fabrics. Cut (15) 1 1/2" squares and (1) 1" x 2 1/2" rectangle from the dark blue hand-dyed fabric.

Place the appropriate square of fabric at one end of the first strip. Press the reverse side of the fabric to the waxy side of the freezer paper, using a dry iron on the wool setting. Fold the pattern back on the first line, releasing the fabric from overlapping the second patch, and trim the fabric so it is an even 1/4" seam allowance across the edge. Align the next appropriate square of fabric with the raw edge you just trimmed but center it on the next space to be covered, not necessarily on the previous fabric square. Fold the paper back again and machine stitch through the fabric right next to the fold. Open the fabric pieces at the seam and press to the waxy side of the paper pattern, avoiding the paper with your iron.

Fold the pattern back on the next line and trim the second patch of fabric so it has an even 1/4" across the edge. Align the next appropriate square, again aligning the raw edge and centering on the next space to be covered. Sew next to the folded paper, press open and to the waxy side of the paper.

As I follow the steps of foundation piecing as I have described, I remember "teaspoon" or "tsp." T — trim the 1/4" seam allowance before adding the next piece; S — stitch the two patches together just next to the folded freezer paper foundation; P — press the seam from the right side, adhering the new patch to the freezer paper foundation. Then fold the paper on the next sewing line and repeat "tsp."

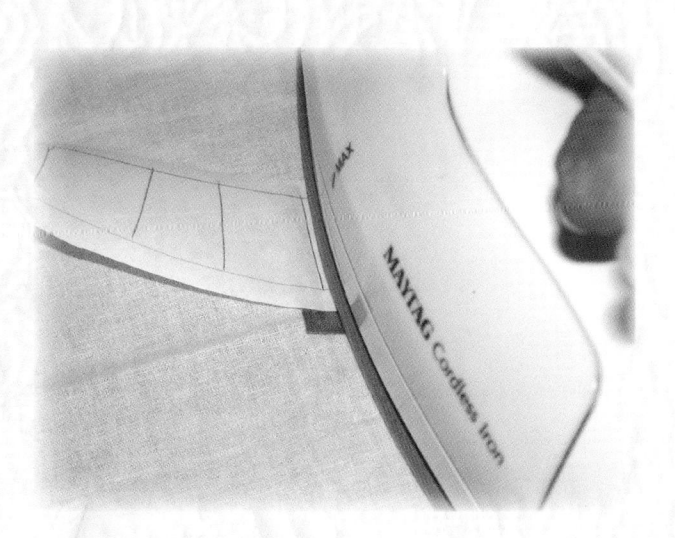

Continue trimming a 1/4-inch seam allowance and adding the next patch until the entire strip is complete. Trim a 1/4-inch seam allowance around the entire row and set aside.

Piece the remaining strips until all the parts to the basket are complete. I hand stitched my strips together (I pieced the appliqué) and then appliquéd the basket to the background.

1/8" Stems

The stems for this block are sewn onto the leaves after they have been attached to the background. If you plan to hand quilt your finished quilt top, you might consider removing the background from behind the leaves before you stitch the stems. Refer to Daisy block (p. 22) for instructions for making the 1/8" stems.

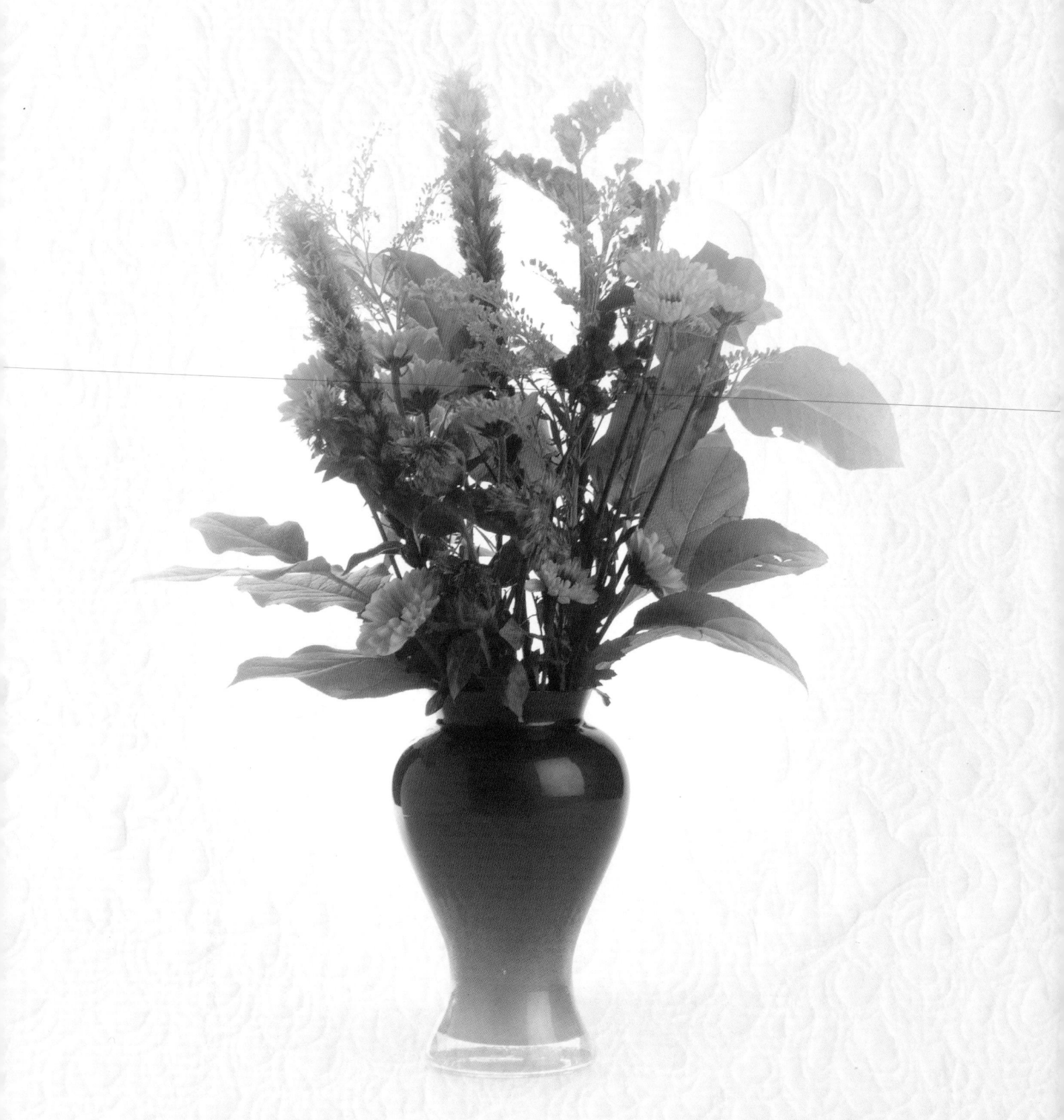

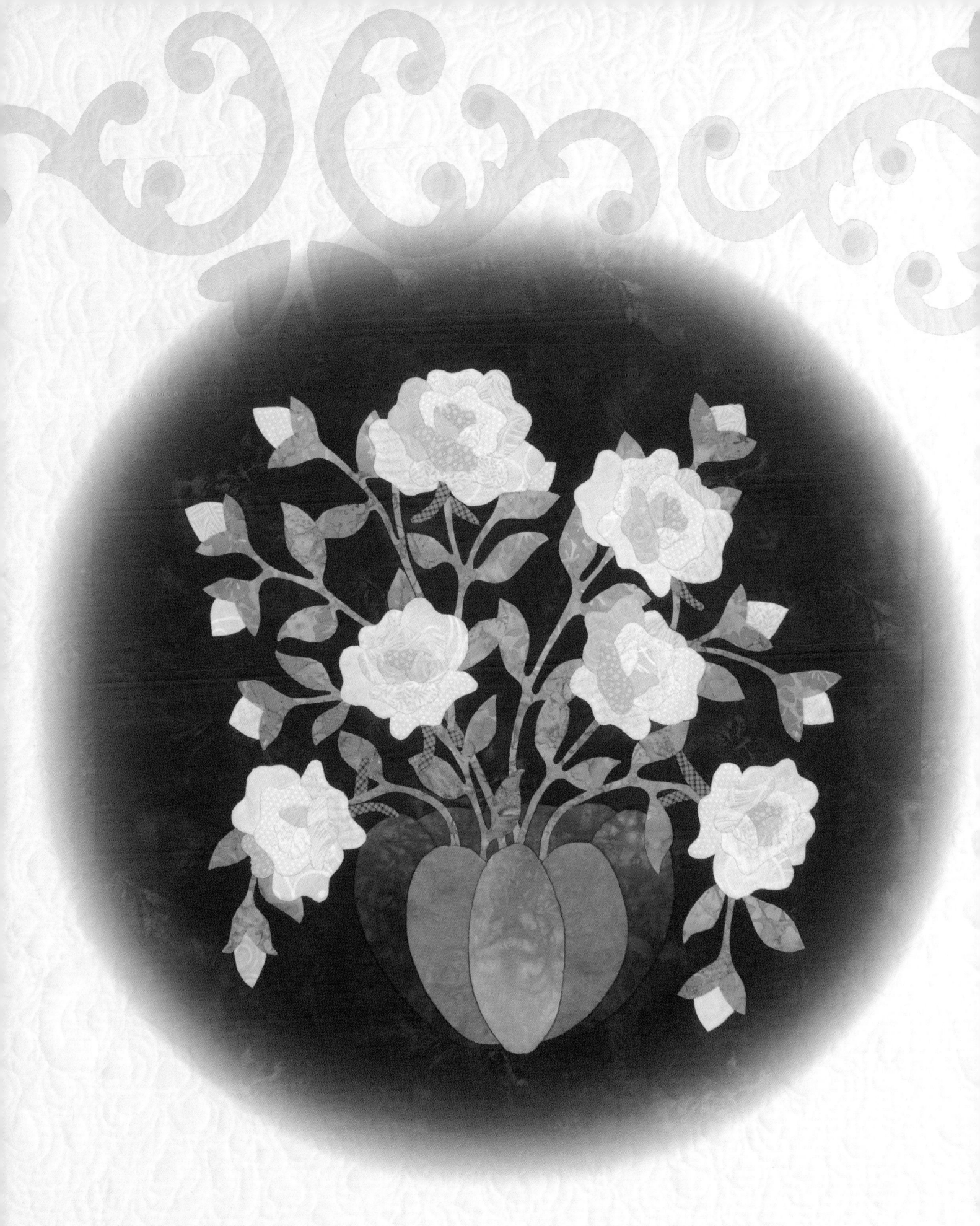

Tea Rose

❧ Appliqué fabric

❀ Fat quarter green for stems / leaf units

❀ 5" x 7" second green for the mature calyxes

❀ (9) 6"x 6" squares of yellow for roses (I used different values from light to medium with a variety of prints)

(Templates begin on page 110)

❧ Leaf / Stem units – Cut-away Appliqué

You will notice the stems are quite narrow and the leaves are attached. This causes a bit of dilemma when it comes to placing the pieces and keeping them in place. If you trim your seam allowances to 3/16th of an inch (or even narrower along the stems) you will have no place to put pins. So, don't cut seam allowance just yet!

Leave about 1/2" around each of the shapes. Go ahead and trace around the templates as you usually do. Place the shape on the background as you usually do and remove the paper template. You will be able to place your basting pins in the excess fabric on the side of the stem you are not stitching – the left side if you are right handed and the right if you are left handed.

To stitch, cut your seam allowance about 2 inches ahead of where you are stitching. As you run out of seam allowance to turn under, trim away more of the excess – about 2 inches ahead. Eventually you will have trimmed away all the excess and completed the appliqué. This is called "cut-away appliqué."

❧ Dimensional Buds

You may want to give your blocks a dimensional effect. Making the rose buds are easy and add grace and charm to your quilt.

While there are several ways to make dimensional buds, my favorite begins with a circle of fabric, about 2 – 2 1/2" in diameter. Fold the circle of fabric in half, reverse side in. Fold the sides toward the middle, in essence folding the half circle in

thirds, and then fold the top layer back on itself just a bit, creating a curled petal. With a running stitch, stitch through all layers and gather. Tuck the bud into the calyx and stitch the calyx to it to secure. A tacking stitch can secure the bud to the background.

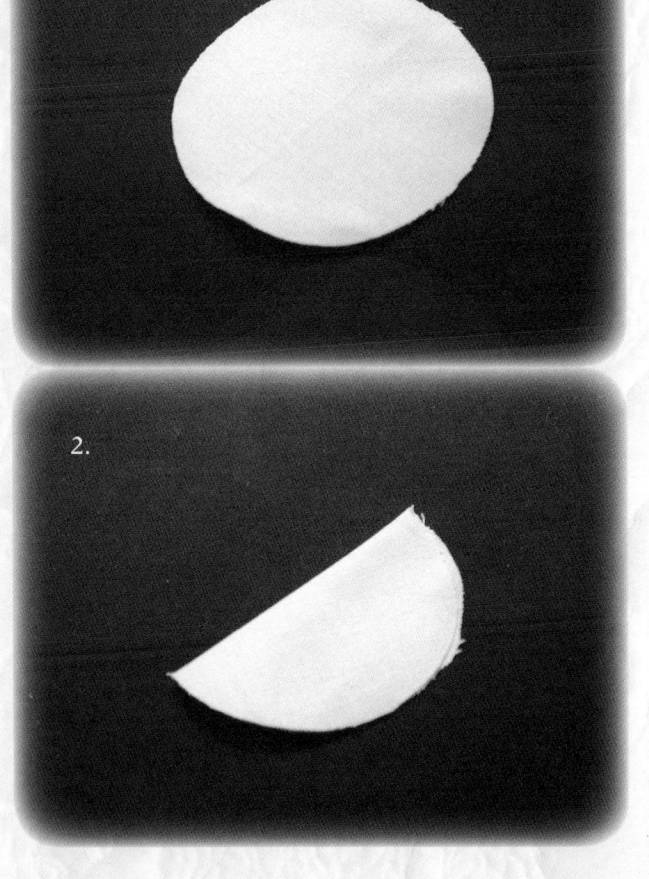

For added interest, consider making a two-toned bud. Begin with two circles of contrasting fabric. Pair them, right sides together and sew through the diameter. Cut the excess fabric from half, leaving a 3/16" seam allowance. Turn right side out and press the fold. When you fold the half-circle into thirds, fold the top edge back on itself, letting the contrasting fabric accent peak out.

1.

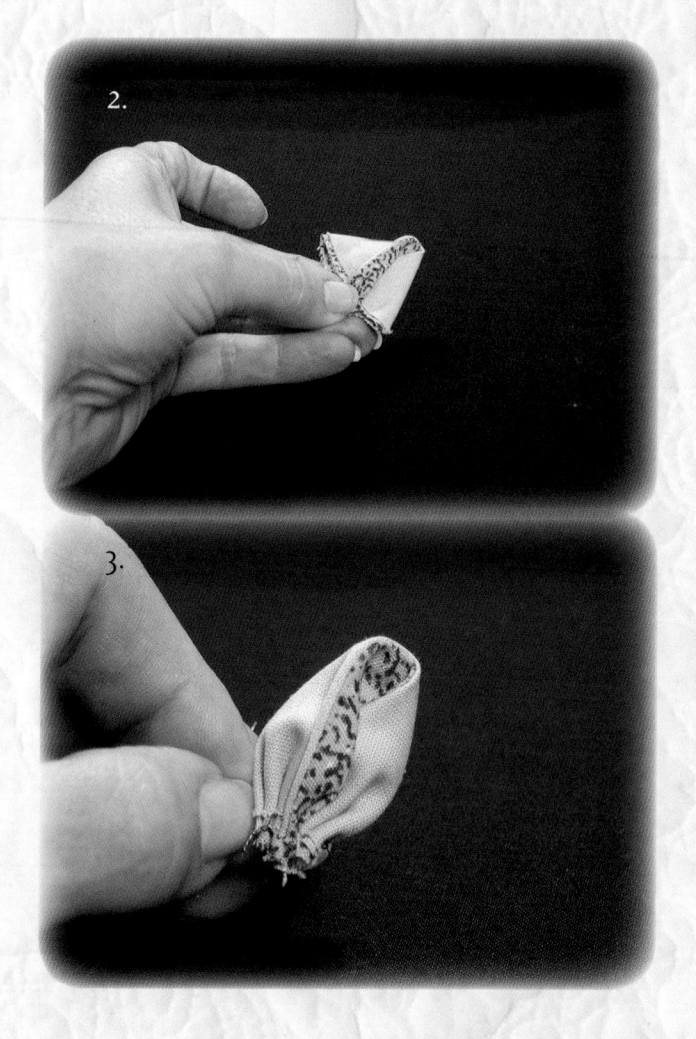

2.

3.

The Borders

⇒ Putting it all together

If you haven't done so already, begin by pressing your blocks, right side down, on a terry towel. The terry towel will maintain the dimensional aspect of your appliqué. Trim the blocks so they are 19 1/2" square. Arrange the blocks as you please, with the wreath in the center. You may wish to refer to the photograph of my quilt for my arrangement. Sew the blocks together in three rows of three blocks each. Press the seam allowance of the first and third row in one direction and the second row in the opposite direction so when you put the rows together your seam intersections will nestle. If you are going to hand quilt your masterpiece, now is the time to remove the background from behind your appliqué if you haven't done so. (Remember, this is why we pieced our appliqué all along.)

Using a pair of Knife-Edge embroidery scissors works the best for me when removing the background from behind my appliqué. One of the blades has a rounded end. When I'm sliding the scissors between the appliqué and the background I don't catch the appliqué fabric, cutting no extra holes. Believe me, before I got these scissors, I sometimes had to add leaves or bugs that were not intended in the design!

⇒ Planning the appliqué border

From the background fabric, cut a 66" length. Remove the selvages and divide the length into (4) equal widths, about 10 1/2" wide.

With a contrasting thread, sew a running (basting) stitch down the center of the length. Fold the strip in half to find the center and just stitch along the crease.

Find the center of the strip and mark the center in the other direction. Again, I used my contrasting thread to baste a running stitch.

Beginning at the center, measure 10" in both directions and mark. These marks will correspond to the seams that connect the center block to the corner blocks.

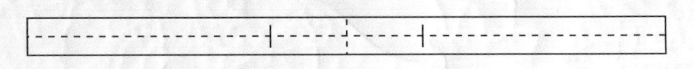

Measure 20" from the new lines and mark again. Mark the center of these segments as well. Your grid on the border strips should look like the figure below.

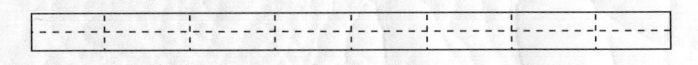

These markings may not exactly reflect the size of your blocks. I did not design appliqué for the corners of the quilt. So you will be spreading the appliqué just a little to account for an inner border that will be added around the blocks. This will also move the appliqué just into the corners a bit. Remember, I don't give my patterns to the Quilt Police so unless you provide a ruler when you exhibit your quilt, no one will know. However, if you have changed the size of your blocks, you may need to change the templates accordingly.

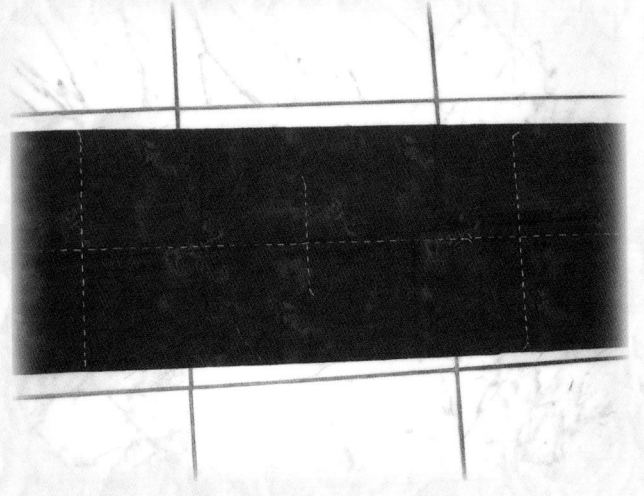

Now you're ready to place the appliqué shapes. The pattern you have for the scroll template is just half the unit. Trace the scroll onto a piece of template plastic. It wouldn't hurt to write the word "left" on the original template. Flip the template over, horizontally, and write the word "right" so you don't get mixed up. Also, transfer the dotted horizontal line to the template.

Refer now to the horizontal mark on the scroll pattern. This line corresponds to the basting stitches you placed down the center of the border strip. When I prepared my appliqué pieces, I folded and creased a 7 1/2" x 19 1/2" rectangle of the scroll appliqué fabric 2 1/2" from the edge, the long way. (This places the fold off-center and corresponds to the dotted line on the scroll template). I folded and creased it again in half the short way. This gave me a placement grid. I placed the plastic template I made of the scroll design so the horizontal placement line aligned with the long center crease. I placed the scroll template so it was 1/4" from the short center crease and traced. (Use a light marker on dark fabric and a dark marker on light fabric.) Then flip the scroll template and repeat on the other side of the short center crease, 1/4" from the short center crease.

Next I placed the rectangle of appliqué fabric on the border strip. I began with the center segment and aligned the creases in the appliqué fabric with the basting stitches on the border strip. I placed a few pins to keep the fabric from shifting and then thread-basted the appliqué fabric to the border

strip. I ran a single running stitch through the center of the appliqué shape. (I usually pin-baste but felt I would be losing pins constantly with all the manipulation I would be doing to the border strip as I stitched.)

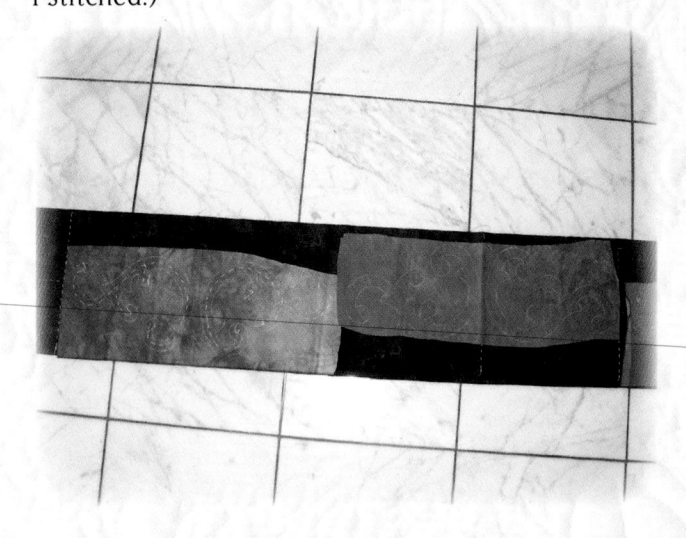

After I had the center scrolls appliquéd in place I repeated with the two on either side. Please note, the design calls for the center scroll design to be flipped so the center scrolls face the opposite direction of the ones on the end of the strip. I had three borders completely stitched before I realized I had forgotten to flip the center design and had to redo them! Once I had all three scroll appliqué pairs basted in place I went back and cut the seam allowance. I used my 4" knife edge embroidery scissors so I was confident I wouldn't catch my border fabric as I cut the excess away.

Use your favorite method to do the appliqué. I know I've mentioned this before, but I prefer needleturn appliqué. Refer to page 10 for directions in this appliqué method. However, use whatever technique works best for you.

The next step is to go back and add the hearts and "drop" design. Place a 5" x 7" rectangle of template plastic over the pattern that includes the hearts as well as some of the scroll design. Trace the outside edge of the scroll set (closest to the hearts) and the hearts. Leave the "drop" for later. Adding the edge of the scroll set gives you a placement guide. (Template is on page 115.)

With a craft knife, cut out the hearts very carefully, cutting a line's width outside the tracing to accommodate for the turn-under line. Discard the cutouts. (You could also cut the lines that represent the scroll to make placement even easier.) It is the window you will be working with. Now, trace sets of the hearts directly onto the right side of the heart appliqué fabric. Use the "window" with the scroll markings for placing the appliqué fabric on your borders sets. Pin or thread baste in place and then cut your seam allowance. If you find it easier for placement, you may wish to make a vinyl placement overlay of that center section of the design.

After the hearts are appliquéd, you can make your "drop" template. Since they are all the same, you can make this template from the template plastic, too. Trace the template onto the right side of the blue fabric and cut out seam allowance. Place the "drop" by using your overlay or you can just "eyeball it" if you are confident.

The blue circles on the scroll designs are made with a Mylar washer form I bought at the hardware store. (Refer to page 32 for the instructions for making circles using the Mylar washers.)

You can freeform stitch the circles, if you like — that is, without a Mylar washer. Choose the appropriate size template from a circle template and trace the circle directly onto the right side of the circle appliqué fabric. Trim the seam allowance and stitch to the scroll designs.

But if you want to make "perfect" circles, use the washers. You can cut them yourself using sandpaper or Mylar template plastic, but it sure is easier to find a supplier of the washers and just buy a bunch. You have 8 circles per scroll set (12 sets) so you'll be making a bunch of circles - 96. I like to have plenty of the forms so I can make a bunch at once, minimizing my running back and forth to the ironing board.

I designed this quilt to actually have two borders. The first border is meant to separate the appliqué of the blocks from the appliqué of the border. Cut (6) 2 1/2" strips from the background fabric. Cut (2) of the strips into (2) 2 1/2" x 22" segments so you'll have (4) shorter strips. Sew each of the shorter strips to the end of each of the (4) longer strips so you'll have a total of (4) 2 1/2" x 63" strips. (Note: if your fabric is not 42" wide after you remove your selvages, you may have to cut another 2 1/2" strip of fabric and add an extra piece to two of the stitched strips to make them long enough for your quilt top.)

Determine the inside edge of your appliquéd border strips. (Refer to the photograph of my quilt for placement.) Sew one of the pieced 2 1/2" strips to the inside edge of each of the appliquéd border strips. (Remember they are slightly shorter than the appliqué border strips so center them.) If you press two of the seam allowances toward the appliqué strip and two toward the 2 1/2" strip, these seams will nest together when you sew the corners in the next step. (Think opposing seams in a 9-Patch block.)

☙ Finishing the Quilt Top

Mitered corners

Measure through the vertical center of the quilt top and divide that number in half. Make a note of the measurement. Find the center of the quilt top edges and mark.

On the edge of one of the border strips, find the center basting mark and measure out from the center to the measurement you noted in the

paragraph above. Place a pin 1/4" less than that measurement. In other words, if your quilt top measured 61 1/2", the number you wrote down was 30 3/4". So you would make a mark on the border strip 30 1/2" from the center in both directions.

Repeat with a second border.

Pin the border strips to the sides of the quilt top, matching the center marks first. The end marks will correspond to 1/4" from the end of the quilt top. Pin the remainder of the border strip in place, easing as needed. Sew the border strips with a 1/4" seam allowance, beginning and ending 1/4" from the end of the quilt top's edges. Backstitch for security.

Measure through the horizontal center of the quilt top without the borders added. Again, divide that number in half and make a note. Find the center of the remaining two border strips and mark the center and the ends as you did with the first two strips. Sew the strips to the quilt top and bottom, backstitching for security.

There are several ways to achieve the mitered corner. Any one of them will give you successful results. Choose your favorite method or you might try the one I use. With right sides together, I make a diagonal fold through one corner of the top. I line up the border strips very evenly along their seams and I pin to secure. Using a ruler, I extend the "line" created by the diagonal fold and mark the diagonal line on the reverse side of the border strip. Beginning at the outside corner and stitching toward

the inside of the miter, I stitch along my drawn line, making sure the seams between the first and second border match. When I open this up I have a perfectly mitered corner. I press the seams open (notice that I "press," I do not "iron") and cut away the excess, leaving a 1/4" seam allowance. I repeat this on the remaining 3 corners.

A rule-of-thumb I often follow for determining my quilting designs is as follows: If the quilt top is defined by a majority of angles, such as triangles, squares, and rectangles, the quilting design should be soft, i.e. curves, cables, etc. If the top is defined by curves, such as in appliqué, the quilting design should back up those curves with angles, i.e. diagonal grids, and channels. If a space is void of angles or curves, such as blank spaces or alternate blocks, my quilt design should have both, i.e. feathers and grids.

The shelves are overflowing with books written on the subject of quilting. I'm certainly not able to tell you here everything about designing the quilting patterns, but my personal rule-of-thumb may give you some place to start.

My quilt was machine quilted by Kelly Ashton of Overland Park, Kansas. We planned a grid, filling every other square in with quilting, creating a "checker board" effect.

Take a look at Linda's quilt on page 73. Linda is an expert quilter and is especially gifted in the white-on-white wholecloth genre. I had talked her into quilting a Lone Star with the appliqué patterns as a wholecloth. The mistake we made was using such a dark background with relatively dark thread. She used different colors of thread but they disappeared. Using a heavier thread such as perle cotton or a lighter background would have been more successful.

⇒ Quilting

Appliqué often looks best if each appliqué shape is outlined by quilting stitches. The quilting seems to bring out the dimension of the appliqué and enhances the design.

✤ Piping

You may wish to add piping to accent the binding. I used a nylon chord (#18) that was very thin and 3/4" wide straight-grain strip of an accent fabric. There are a variety of methods for piping. I must say, I still use the same method I learned MANY years ago. I use my zipper foot to sew the filled strip of fabric to the quilt top, making sure I don't stretch it or it will distort the finished quilt. You can use four strips, one for each side, or one continuous strip. I think the corners are crisper and neater with the four strips.

If you press a crease into the piping fabric, you may find it easier to keep the fabric straight. Sometimes the fabric strip will twist around the chord as you are sewing. Folding the strip, reverse side in, and pressing creates a channel that the chord will nestle into.

I squared my quilt top by marking the edge with a marker when I was ready to put the piping and binding on my quilt. The act of quilting can distort the quilt some, so I mark my edge. While some quilters will trim the excess backing and batting at this point, I do not. I simply draw the edge. It is this marked line to which I match the raw edge to the piping or binding. I save the trimming for when the binding has been added.

I like to make four separate piping strips, one per side, instead of one continuous strip that will

be attached all the way around the quilt, turning the corners. I have done it both ways and I like the look of the sharp corners created by the four strips better than the turned corners. I start on one side and add each side in order — unlike adding borders when I add the borders on opposing sides before adding the remaining two sides. When I get around to the beginning, I tuck the final strip under the beginning of the first so each corner is identical.

With a zipper foot and the needle moved to the far left position I am ready to begin. First, to add the piping, I pull the needle one position to the right. I want the stitching to be next to the piping, but I'm leaving space to move the needle even closer to the piping when adding the binding, thus hiding the first row of stitching within the seam allowances of the piping and binding.

Sew the piping to the quilt top by guiding the zipper foot right next to the chord within the fabric strip. I don't pin the piping to the quilt top, but guide it as I stitch. I am also careful not to stretch the piping strip as I work.

Once the piping has been stitched in place, move the needle again to the far left position and sew the binding to the quilt top, again matching the raw edge to the drawn edge of the quilt top. At this point I still do not trim the excess. But if you want to trim before adding the binding, there is a tool that would come in very handy. It is a Plexiglas "ruler" that has a groove cut in 1/4" from the edge and 3/8" from the edge. This groove fits right over

the piping and lets you trim an equal distance from the piping all the way around. I recommend that you choose the 3/8". This will assure a filled binding when you fold the binding to the back to finish.

⇒ Binding

Depending on the batting you have chosen, or the loft, that is thickness, you will cut strips for your binding either 2 1/2" wide or 2 1/4" wide. On rare occasions, I actually cut my binding 2 1/8" wide, but each time I have found it to be just the tiniest bit too narrow. So I recommend no less than 2 1/4" wide strips. To determine the number of strips that you will need, measure the top and a side, multiply by two (to get the total circumference of your quilt top) and then divide by 40 (the average usable length of a strip when cut selvage to selvage, after the selvage is removed). Naturally a partial strip should be counted as a whole strip. So if the number you get is, say, 5.666, then you would cut 6 strips.

To determine the amount of fabric needed for the binding, multiply the number of strips that are needed by 2 1/2" and then round up about 1/8 yard. This gives you enough to straighten the fabric before you begin cutting the strips and even make a mistake. (I always multiply by 2 1/2" even if I'm going to make the strips 2 1/4" wide.) So, say I need 6 strips. That's 15 inches. I'll round up to 1/2 yard (18") and that will give me another strip should I need it. If I had needed exactly 18" I would still have rounded up so that I would have extra, just in case.

Remove the selvages and sew the strips together on the bias across the tails, not through them.

Trim the excess so that you have a 1/4" seam allowance and press the seam open. This will help to eliminate bulk. Press the entire strip in half (the full length), reverse side in. Now you're ready to bind your quilt.

I do not trim away the excess batting or backing before adding the binding. But I do make sure that the corners are square. Using your 12 1/2″ square ruler, mark the corners square if they have been distorted at all. When sewing the binding to the quilt, let this line guide you in the corners, not the edge of the quilt top.

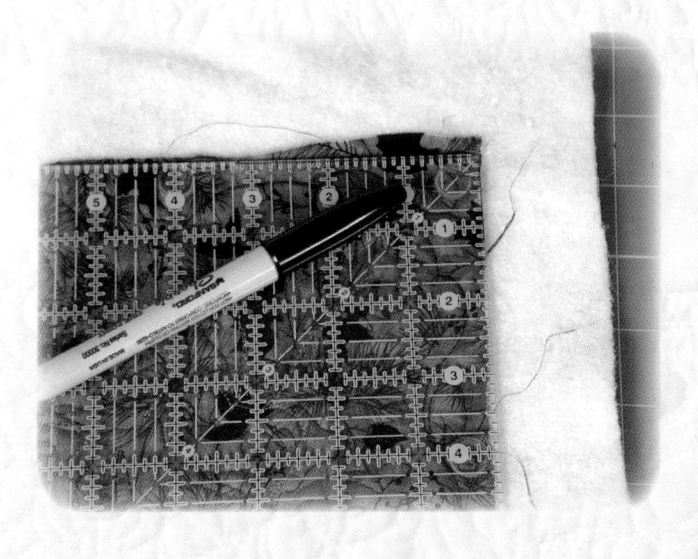

Fit your sewing machine with your walking foot. Move your needle to the far right position so that it is 1/4″ to 3/8″ from the edge of the foot. The edge of the foot will be your sewing guide. At this point I have not removed any of the excess batting or backing. I wait to do that after the binding is attached. I also increase the length of my stitches just a bit since I'm going to be sewing through more thickness than when I piece.

Begin in the center of a side. Leaving a 10-12″ tail, sew the binding, raw edges to the edge of your quilt top or the marking you made for the square corner. Sew to the corner but not all the way through the corner. Stop the same distance from the corner that your needle is from the edge of the quilt, 1/4″ to 3/8″. Pull the quilt out from under the needle and foot and turn the quilt so that you will be sewing the next edge. Fold the binding at a 45-degree angle from the stitched part. The raw

edge of the binding and the raw edge of the next side of the quilt top will form a straight line. If not, it's probably because you stitched beyond where you should have. If that's the case, then clip that last stitch or two if needed. This allows you to pull the binding back farther so that you do make that straight line. If it is straight, then fold the binding down over the corner, aligning the raw edge with the new side. Begin sewing again from just off the edge to just before the next corner and repeat.

When you get to the final side, stop sewing about 12-15" from where you began. At this point there are several ways to finish, some appearing bulkier than others. The method I use isn't really that hard once you get the hang of it and it gives me a smooth join without measuring anything. So let me walk you through this slowly. Once you get it, you'll be delighted with the technique.

Bring the two tails together in the middle of the unsewn space. Fold the tails back on themselves so that there is about a 1/8" gap between the two where the folds meet. Make a small clip though all four layers of the binding fabric right where they meet in the center, perpendicular to the raw edge. Be sure that your clip is no deeper than about 1/8". You don't want to clip through where you will be sewing your seam.

(See photo at top of page 61.)

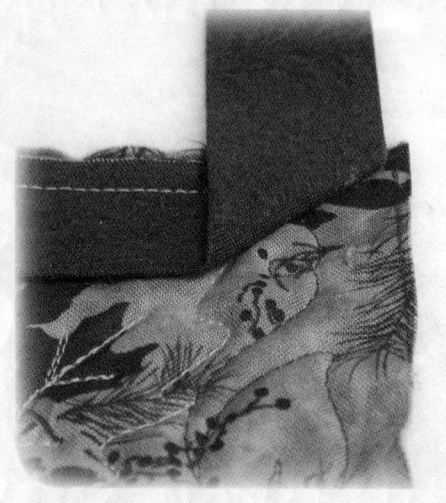

Now place your quilt on your table so that the edge on which you are working is right in front of you and the rest of the quilt is across the table. Open the left tail. The right side will be toward the quilt top and the reverse side will be showing. Place your left hand, palm up, on the quilt top behind the open binding (the binding is between you and your hand). With your right hand, flip the tail over, toward your hand, so that the reverse side of the binding is now in your hand and the right side is facing up. Angle the end of the tail toward the center of your quilt.

Open the right tail so that the reverse side is facing up and angle it toward the center of the quilt top. Now place the right tail on top of the left tail. Cross them at a 45-degree angle to each other. Match the clips you made so that the correct placement occurs. Place a pin to hold the matched points in place. You will be sewing across the tails, so place your pins perpendicular to the sewing line.

Press the seam open and trim for a 1/4" seam allowance. Fold the binding again, reverse side in, as you had in the beginning and press. Align the raw edges to your quilt top and finish sewing the binding to the top between the point where you began and ended. You should notice that the binding is flat and smooth!

Once the binding is attached you are ready to remove the excess batting and backing. I always want to be sure that the batting completely fills my binding. To that end I cut the excess, leaving about 1/8" extending past the raw edge of the binding. I'll admit it, I use scissors. I really don't have a space to lay out my quilt so as to use a rotary cutter and ruler. But the rotary cutter would really work faster!

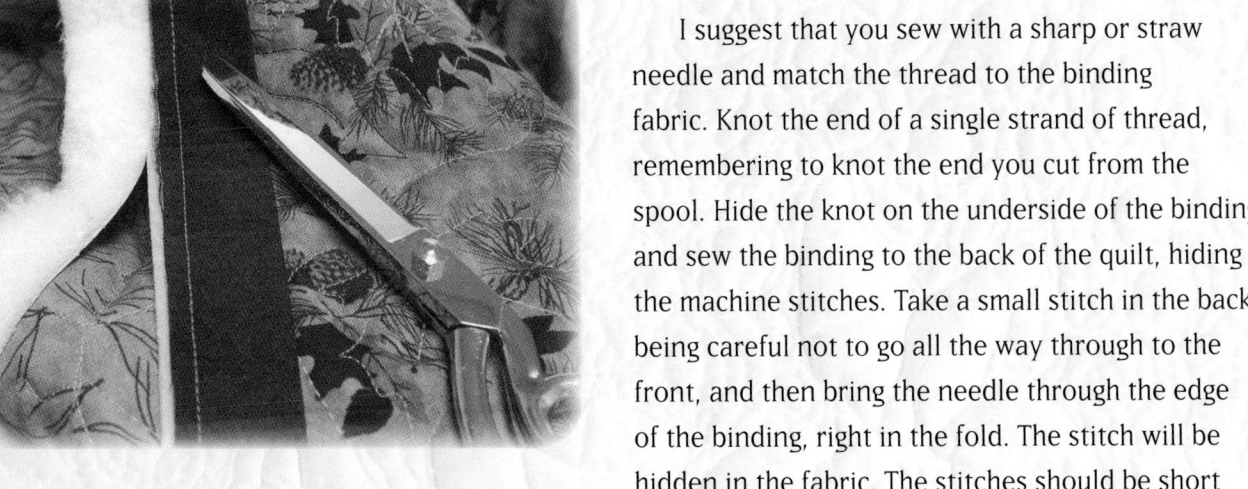

I suggest that you sew with a sharp or straw needle and match the thread to the binding fabric. Knot the end of a single strand of thread, remembering to knot the end you cut from the spool. Hide the knot on the underside of the binding and sew the binding to the back of the quilt, hiding the machine stitches. Take a small stitch in the back, being careful not to go all the way through to the front, and then bring the needle through the edge of the binding, right in the fold. The stitch will be hidden in the fabric. The stitches should be short and close together so the binding is secure.

Fold the finished edge around the raw edge to the back, just covering the machine stitching, to complete the binding. You won't have to pin all of the binding to the back, but you will find that securing some as you're working will keep the fabric from stretching. Some quilters will use pins, pinning in the direction they stitch so they don't prick knuckles. My favorite method uses "binding clips" that have, for a previous generation, acted as hair clips! You will find these marvelous tools at your local quilt shop.

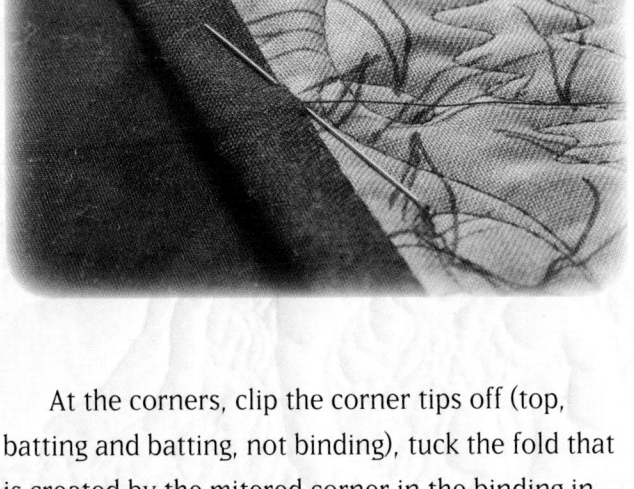

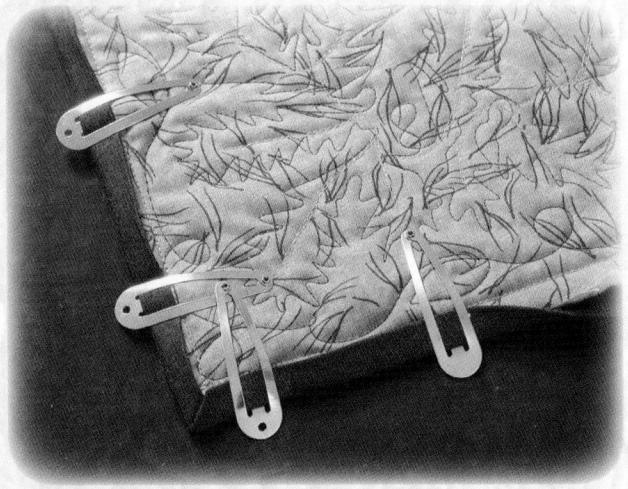

At the corners, clip the corner tips off (top, batting and batting, not binding), tuck the fold that is created by the mitered corner in the binding in the opposite direction of the fold on the front side. This will distribute the bulk so that the corner is smoother. If the binding gaps in the corner, stitch the fold, both front and back. This will make an even neater corner.

I used my embroidery software and embroidery module for my machine to create my label. I pieced it into the backing of my quilt to make it part of the back instead of applying it to the back.

Your final step is to document the quilt with a label on the back. With the advent of the home embroidery machines, elaborate labels are being created with little effort. If you don't own the embroidery module with your sewing machine, you can appliqué a design, use fabric paint to paint a design or colored permanent pens to draw the design. You can even use your computer to create and print your label on specially treated fabric.

I hope this gives you some ideas for completing your own Pots de Fleurs quilt!

The most important element, though, is the information about you and the quilt. Include the title of your quilt, your name, the date of completion - the date of starting your quilt, if you dare! — from where came the pattern, where you were when you created your quilt (city and state) and any other information you want your descendents to know about you and your quilt. When the label is created and attached to the back of the quilt, the quilt is complete.

Pots de Fleurs in Taupes

Wall Quilt

Made by Carol Nash, Overland Park, Kansas

67" x 24"

❧ Fabric

- ✿ 2 yards (block backgrounds, sashing, and border)
- ✿ 5/8 yard contrasting (flange and binding)
- ✿ 2 yards (backing)
- ✿ Assorted fabrics for appliqué

Choose three blocks for this wall quilt. Carol chose the Tulip, Rose and Iris blocks. You'll find

instructions with the individual patterns. Remove the selvages from the length of the 2-yard piece of fabric. Cut (3) 22" squares from the length of the fabric.

When the appliqué blocks are complete and trimmed to 20 1/2" square you will add the flange. For each block, cut (2) 1" strips from selvage to selvage. Cut the strips to 1" x 20".

Fold the strips, reverse side in, the length of the

strip and press. Align the raw edges of the flange strips with the raw edge of the blocks. Baste the flange to the block, using a 1/8" seam allowance, taking care not to stretch the flange as you sew. Sew the side flanges on and then the top and bottom.

Cut (4) 2 1/2" strips from the length of the remaining background fabric. Cut two of the strips to (4) 2 1/2" x 20 1/2" strips for sashing and the side borders. Sew the strips to the left side of each of the blocks and to the right side of one of the blocks — the block you have determined to be on the right of the middle block. Sew the three blocks together into a horizontal row of blocks with a 1/4" seam allowance. Press the seam allowances toward the strips.

Measure through the horizontal center of the quilt top. Trim the remaining (2) 2 1/2" strips to that measurement and sew to the top and bottom of the quilt top. Press the seam allowances toward the border strips.

⊰ Finishing

Carol hand quilted her wall quilt. She quilted around each appliqué shape and then used a 1" painters' tape to guide her in the radiating lines in the background. She then rounded the four corners of the quilt. Rounding the corners then requires a bias binding. This is done by cutting your binding strips 2 1/4" or 2 1/2" wide and on the bias and treating them as you would straight-grain strips. The bias allows you to sew the binding smoothly around the corners.

Sew the strips together, end to end. Press the seam allowances open and trim to 1/4". Refer to page 58 for binding instructions.

Bouquet d'ete

Wall Quilt

Made by Tresa Jones, Seneca, Kansas
32" x 32"

*T*resa chose three of her favorite blocks and combined them into one glorious bouquet of summer flowers. Tresa's pattern is provided, beginning on page 116, but you may decide to exchange her favorites for your favorite summer blooms. Please note that Tresa created her flowers as a unit before adding them to the background. A couple of the flowers are the same so the numbering in the templates will reflect this.

Fabric

* 1 5/8 yards appliqué background and corner triangles
* 1/6 yard contrast
* 1 yard backing
* 1/3 yard binding
* Assorted fabrics for appliqué

The fabric Tresa used for her background is directional. She chose to place her bouquet on the straight of grain so when she trimmed her block, she trimmed her block on the bias. This allowed her to maintain the directional aspect of the fabric design. It also occurred to her that the appliqué may be heavy and placing the block on the straight of grain and trimming on the bias, might make the quilt less likely to sag over time while hanging on the wall.

If you don't wish to work with so many bias edges as you put your quilt top together, you may plan to appliqué your bouquet "on point" to begin. Then when you trim the block, you will still be sewing straight-of-grain edges of the block. The density or your quilting will act to reinforce the quilt while it hangs on the wall as well.

Stitch the appliqué to a 25" or 26" square. Once the appliqué is finished, trim the square to 22 1/2" square.

Cut (4) 1" strips, selvage to selvage, from the contrasting fabric. Sub-cut two of the strips to 1" x 22 1/2" and sew to opposite sides of the appliquéd square with a 1/4" seam allowance. Press the seam allowances toward the strips. If you are sewing the strips to bias edges of the block, sew with the bias edges on the bottom, against the feed dogs. This minimizes the stretching that can occur.

Measure through the center of your square, including the contrasting strips. Trim the remaining contrasting 1" strips to that measurement and sew to the remaining edges with a 1/4" seam allowance. Press the seam allowances toward the strips. Again, if you are sewing the strips to bias edges of your block, sew with the bias edges against the feed dogs.

Cut (2) 17" squares for your corner triangles. Cut the squares on the diagonal once for (4) 1/2-square triangles. Sew the triangles along the long edges to the center of your quilt top. Sew with the bias edges of the triangles against the feed dogs and work on opposite edges as you add the triangles to the center square. Trim the excess away after quilting to square the quilt.

Tresa hand quilted her wall quilt. She quilted a chevron design behind the appliqué in the center block and feathered hearts in the corner triangles. I also recommend quilting around each of the appliqué shapes to add dimension to the appliqué.

Chocolate Lily Pillow

Made by Susan Winnie, Arcadia, California • 22" x 22"

✿ Fabric

- 24" square (pillow top)
- 24" muslin (pillow top quilt backing)
- 24" square low loft batting
- 24" x 28" rectangle (pillow back)
- 1/2 yard contrast (binding)
- (2) 1" buttons
- 18" square pillow form
- Additional Fiberfil - optional

Appliqué the Chocolate Lily onto the center of the 24" pillow top square, following the instructions with the pattern. When the appliqué is complete, layer the muslin, batting and appliqué block and quilt the sandwich. Susan machine quilted her quilt top. She stitched around the appliqué and then stitched a 2 1/2" diagonal grid behind the appliqué.

Cut an 11" square of freezer paper. Fold it in half, diagonally. Make a mark about 14" from one corner along the folded edge. This point will represent the outer corner of the pillow. Draw a curved line from the point you marked to the corner that is not folded. It should be a graceful line with one "dip." Place staples near the drawn line. This will stabilize the paper as you cut the paper on the drawn line. Remove the staples and open the folded paper.

Align the straight edge with the center marks you used as you placed the appliqué shapes. (See page 10, "Preparing the Background.") Trace the curved edge onto the quilt top, creating the first corner. You will not need to worry whether the mark will come out as this line will be inside the binding. Rotate the paper and trace the second corner. Keep rotating and tracing the corner until you have a scalloped line around the appliqué. Mark a square on the quilt top, 2" in from the widest point on all four sides. This will make an 18" square centered on the appliqué. The marker you use for this mark will need to come out. A blue washout marker will work as long as you wash your pillow when it is complete. Just spritzing the mark with water may make the line appear to be removed, but the chemicals are still there. The mark will return.

Cut the 24" x 28" pillow backing into (2) 24" x 14" rectangles. Hem one of the long edges of each of the rectangles. Fold the edge 1/2" under and 1/2" again. Press and topstitch to finish. With your sewing machine, make two button holes that will fit your 1" buttons. Make the button holes 6" apart and centered along the finished edge of one of the backing rectangles, 1/2" from and perpendicular to the finished edge. Sew the two buttons about 1 1/2" from the finished edge of the second backing rectangle, 6" apart and centered along the finished edge. Button the two rectangles together and set aside.

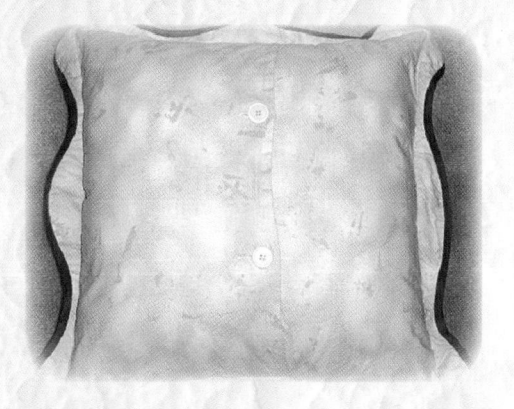

Align the raw edges with the drawn scalloped line you drew. Sew the binding through all layers, taking care not to stretch the binding, easing the raw edges of the binding strip on the inside curves and slightly stretching the raw edges of the binding strip on the outside curves. Refer to page 58 for instructions on joining the binding. After the binding has been attached, cut away the excess and then finish the binding by hand stitching the folded edge to the back of the pillow, covering the machine stitching with the folded edge.

Place the pillow backing, right side – button side – down, on a table surface. Place the pillow top, right side up on top of the backing, centering the top so the buttons are in the center of the pillow back. Pin through all the layers to secure and sew through all the layers on the 18" square you marked on the pillow top.

If the pillow form doesn't fill the corners of the pillow, you might consider adding a little Fiberfil to the corners.

Because the edge of the pillow is scalloped, you will need to make bias binding. Cut 2 1/4" or 2 1/2" bias strips. Sew enough strips, end to end, so you have about 95" of binding. Press the seam allowances open and trim to 1/4". Fold the pieced strip the length of the strip, reverse side in, and press the fold. And I do mean "press." Ironing will stretch the bias strip and you want to be careful that doesn't happen.

Gallery

Fleurs Pastelles
79" x 79"
Made by Mindy Peterson, Springhill, Kansas
Quilted by Sandy Gore, Liberty, Missouri

Embroidery in Blue

70" x 70"

Made by Barb Fife, Overland Park, Kansas
Bluework by Pearle Gerdes, Auburn, Nebraska
Quilted by Freda Smith, Kansas City, Kansas

Lilies
36" x 36"
Made by Eugena Turner
Independence, Missouri

Alaskan Mountain Harebell Wholecloth Quilt
40" x 40"
Made by Linda Birch Mooney, Shawnee, Kansas

Purple Iris
24" x 24"

Made by Nancy Kerns, Skillman, New Jersey
Quilted by Karen Thompson, Newtown, Pennsylvania

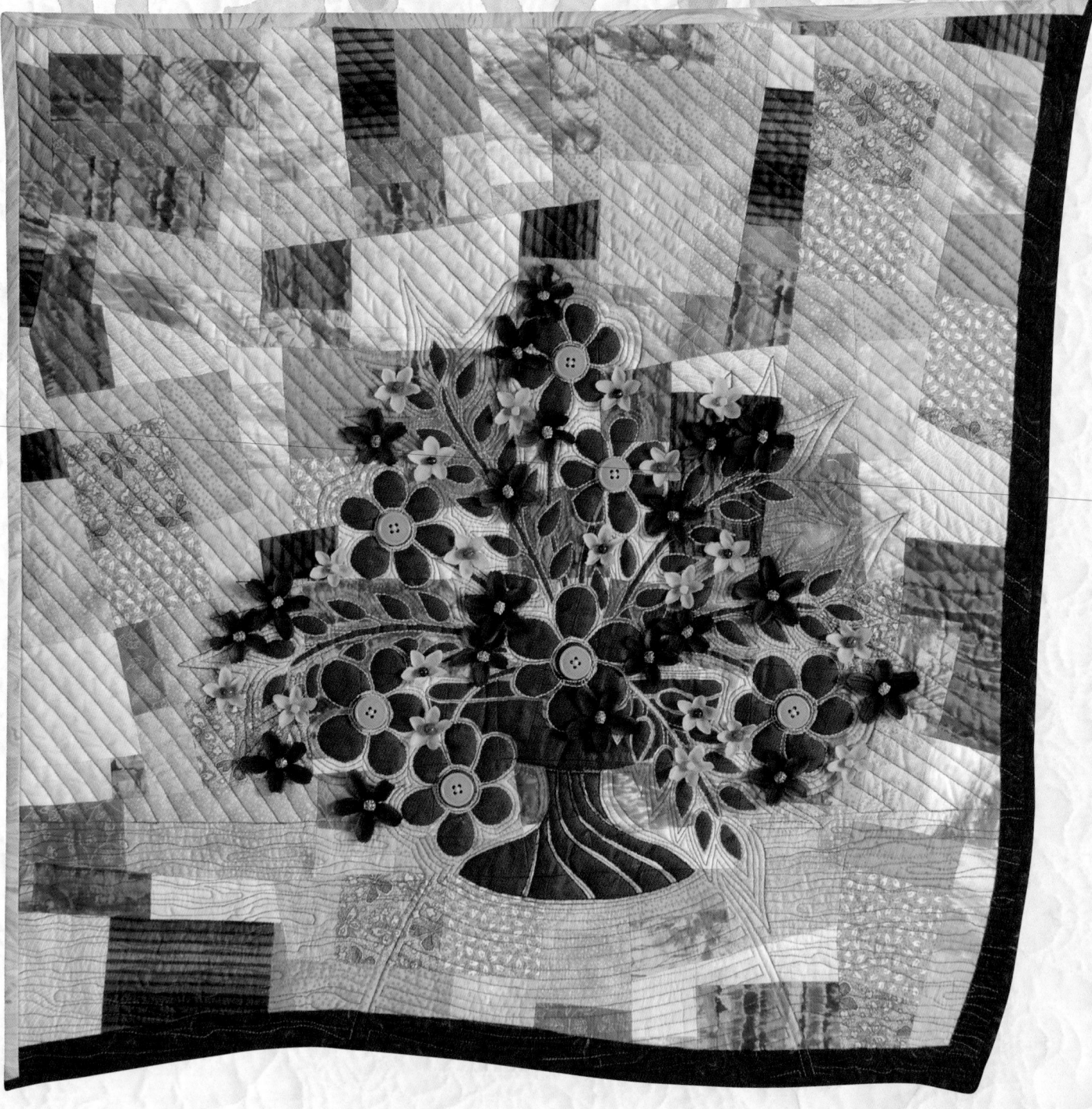

Upsy Daisy

25" x 25"

Made by Karen G. Fisher, Tucson, Arizona

Tulips
13 1/2" x 13 1/2"
Made by Mindy Peterson, Springhill, Kansas

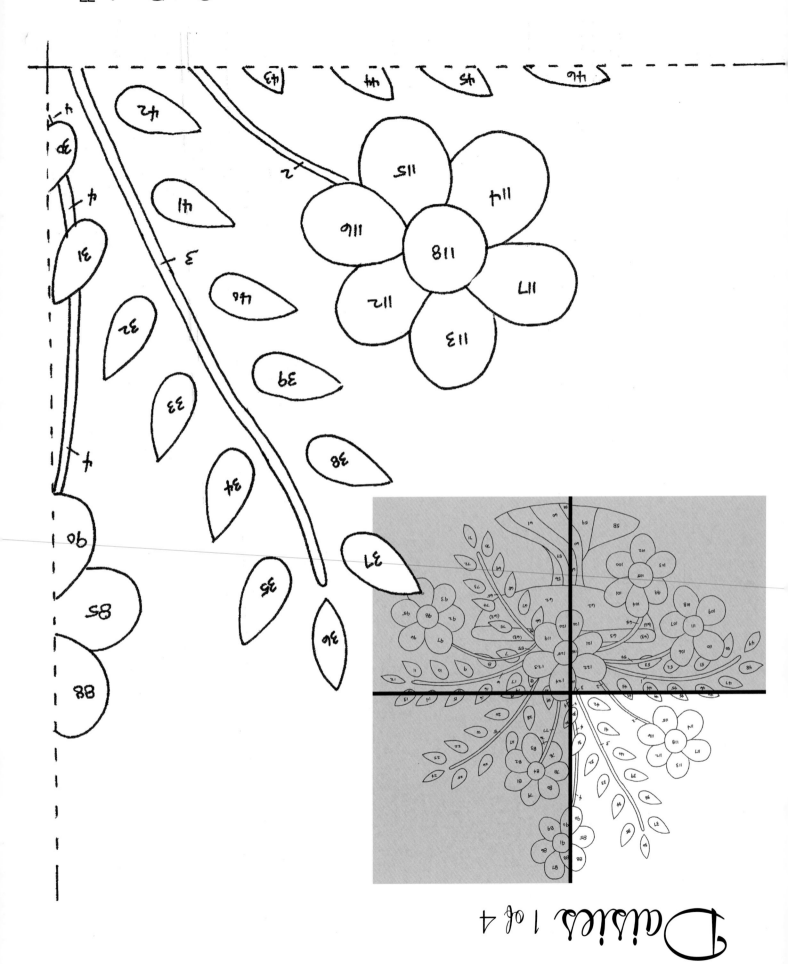

Daisies 1 of 4

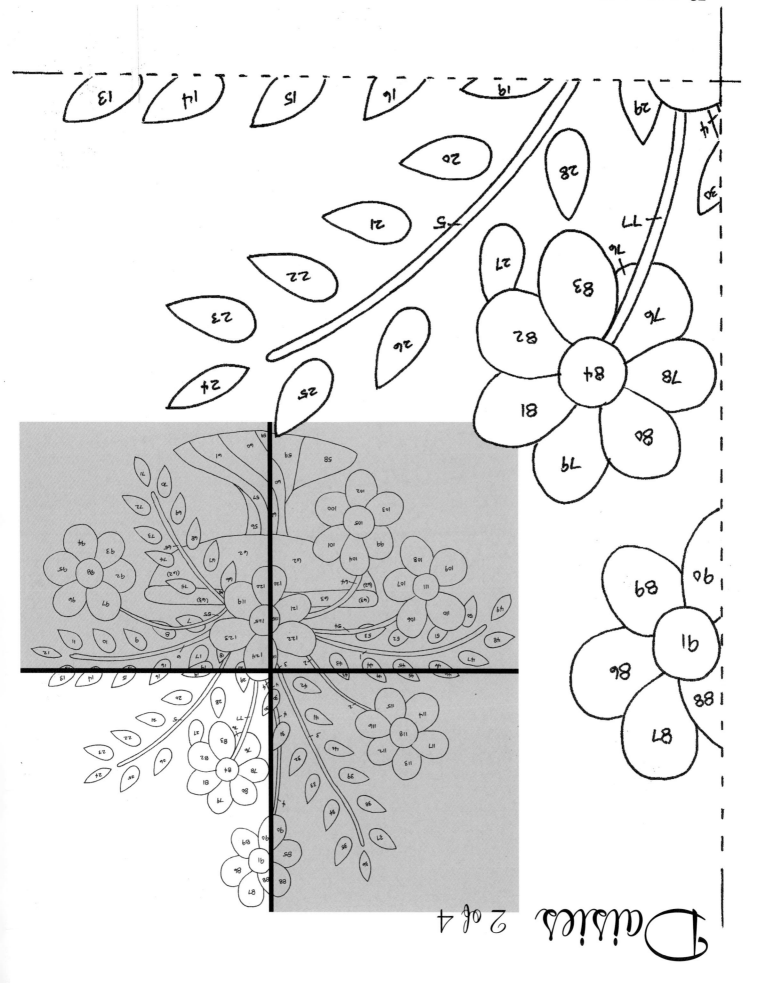

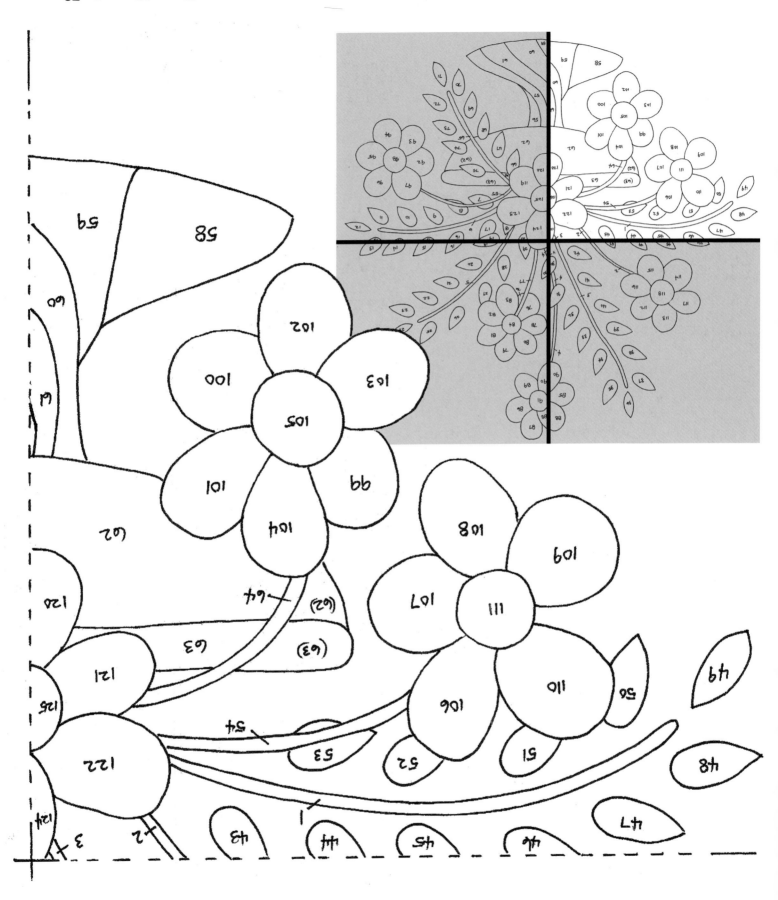

Dahlia 3 of 4

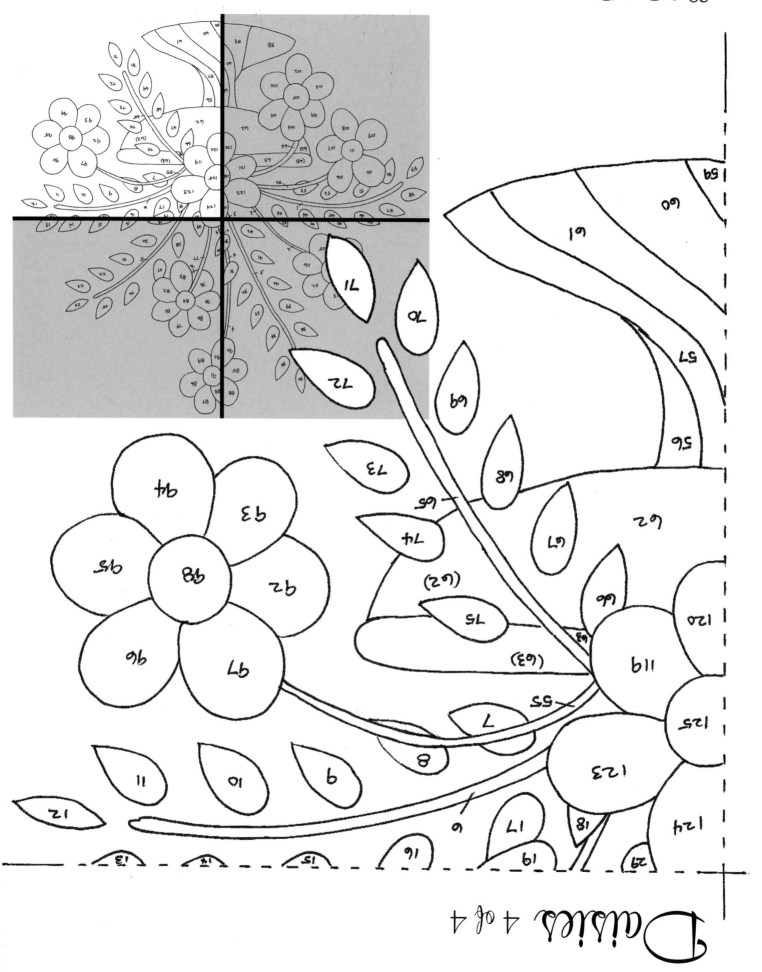

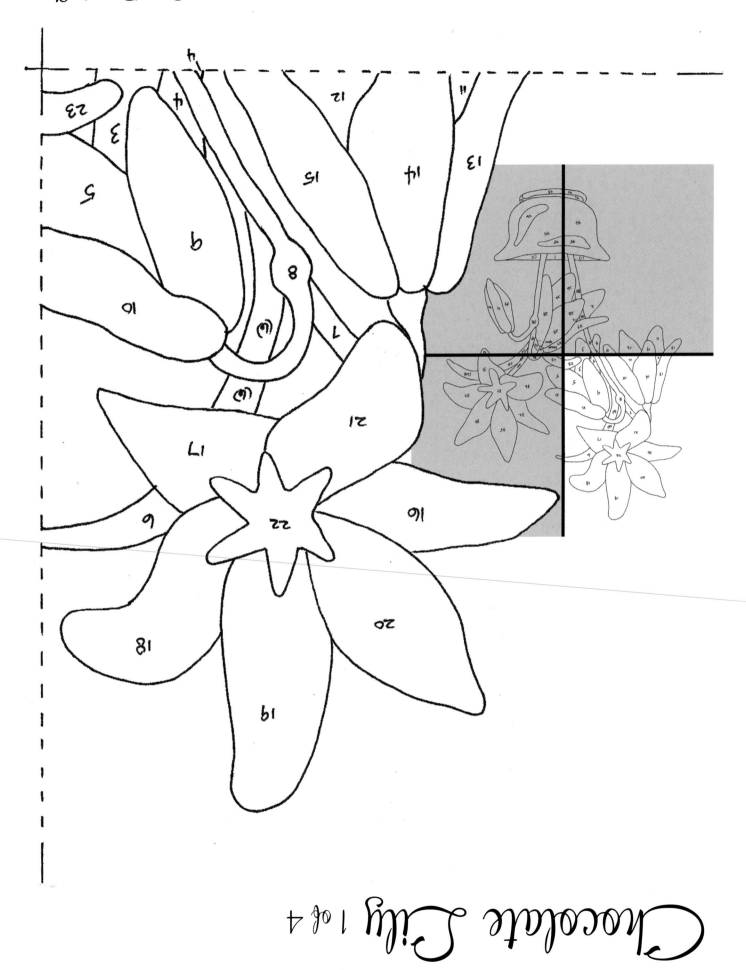

Chocolate Lily 1 of 4

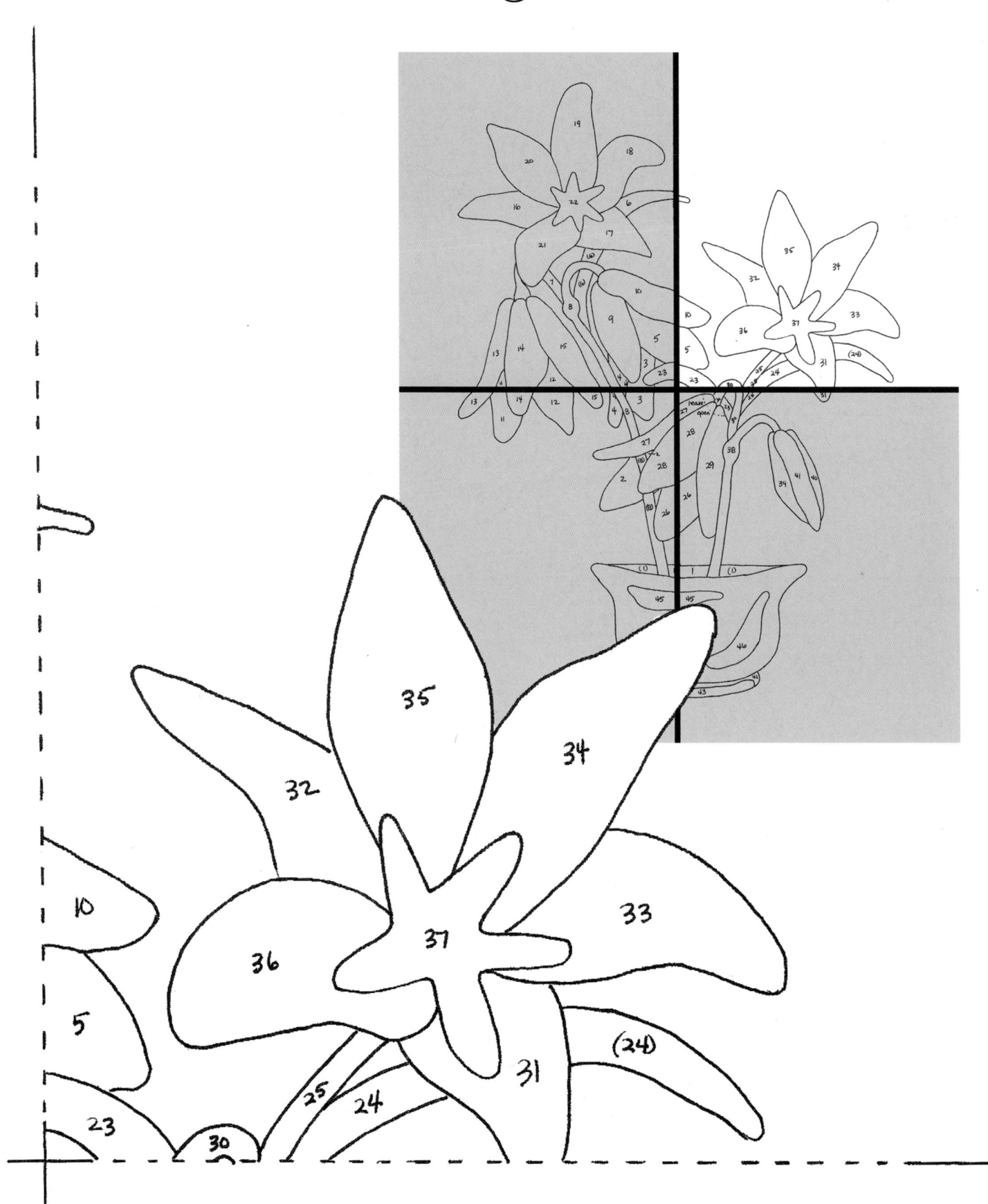

Chocolate Lily 3 of 4

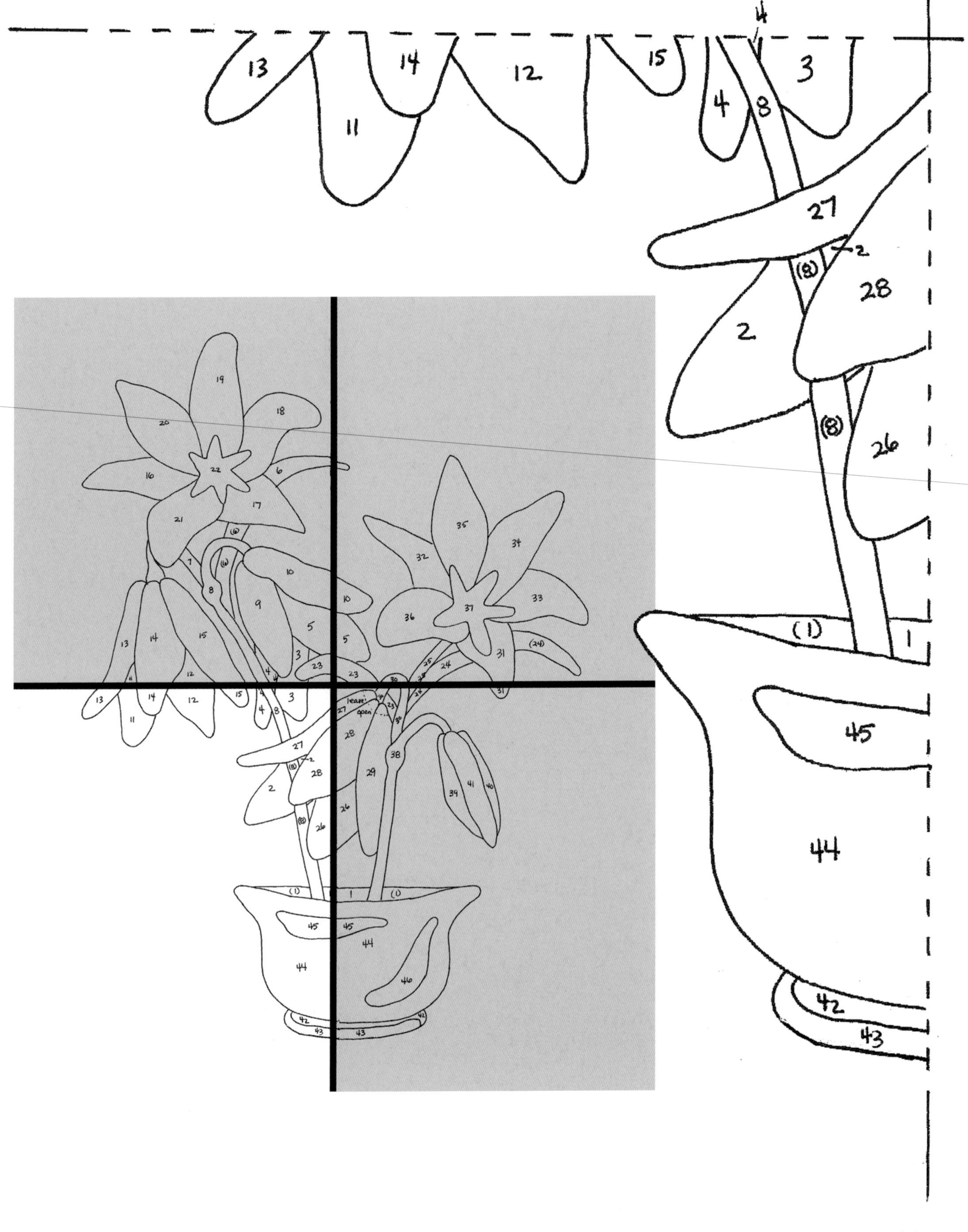

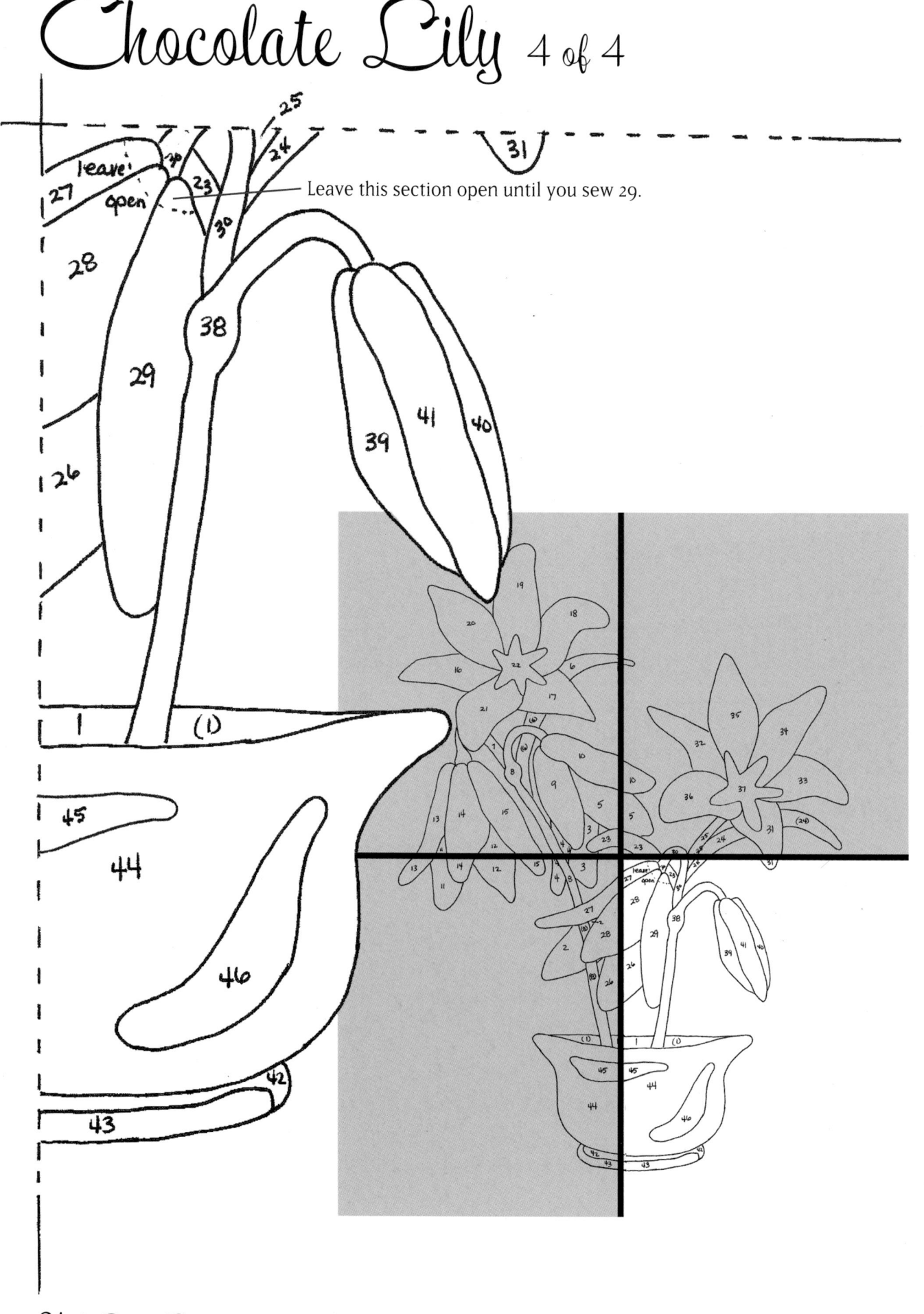

Leave this section open until you sew 29.

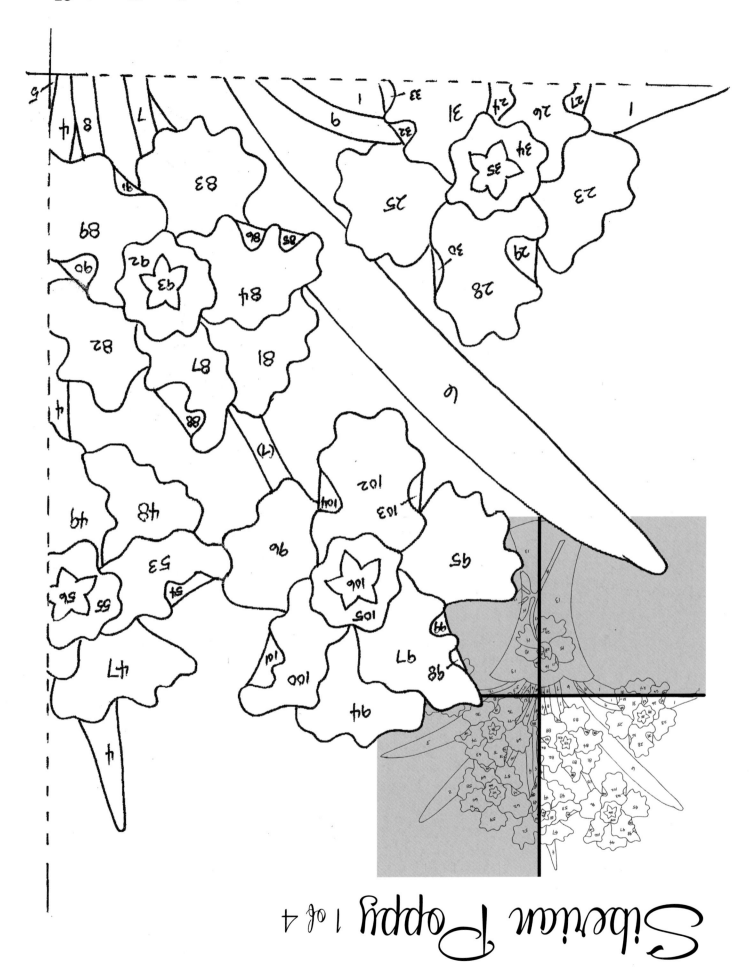

Siberian Poppy 1 of 4

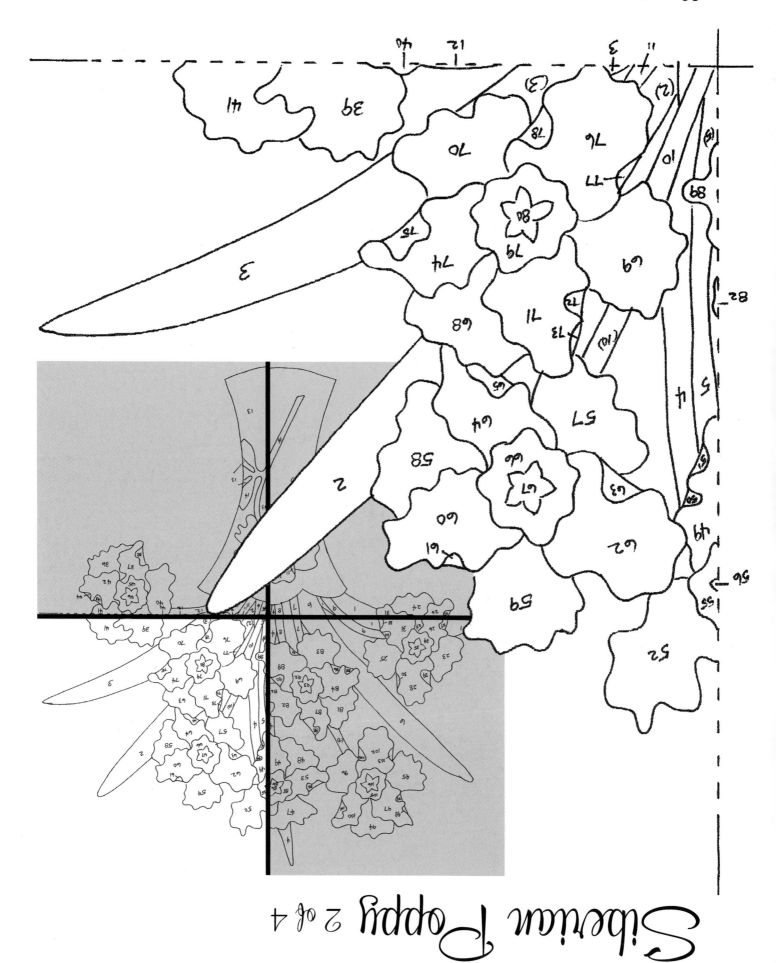

Siberian Poppy 2 of 4

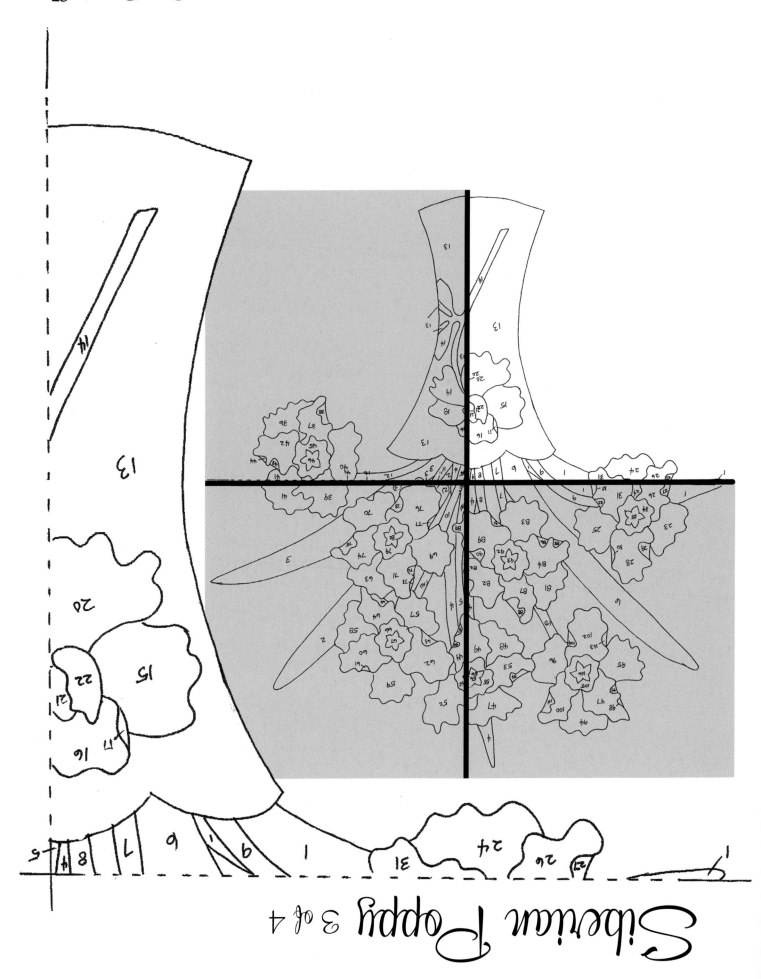

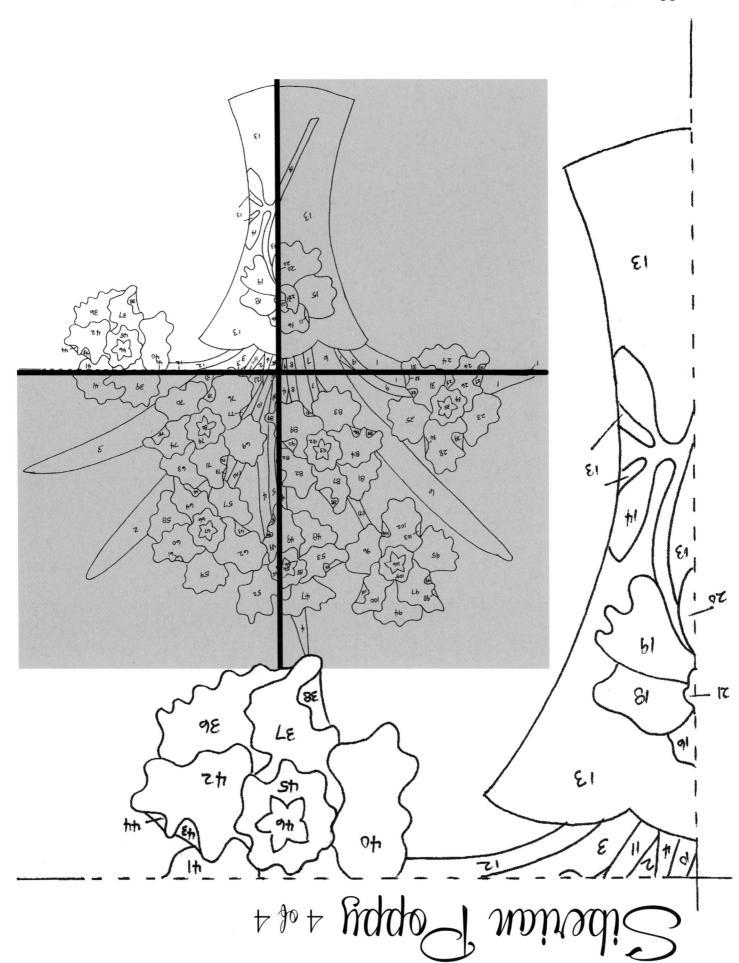

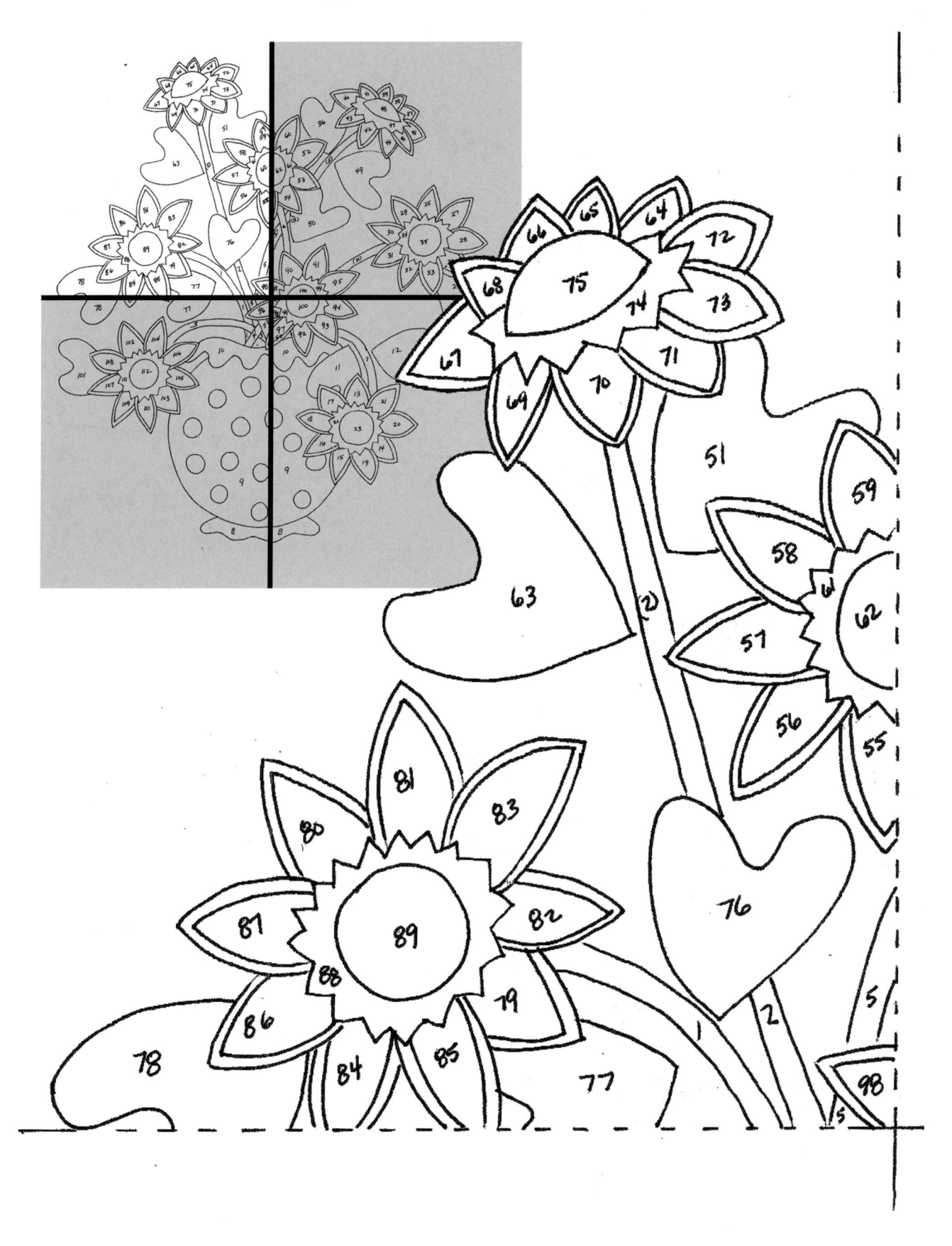

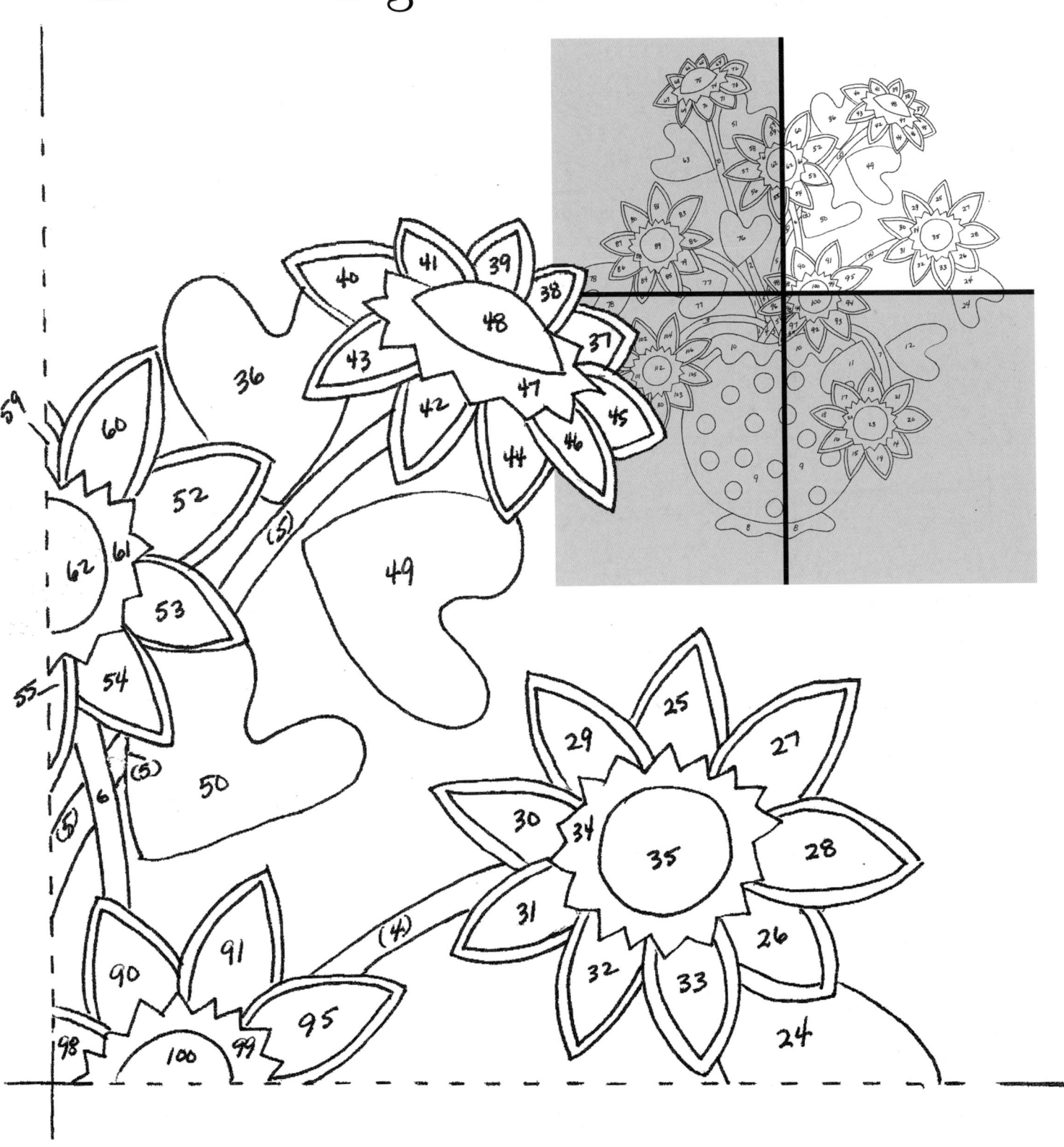

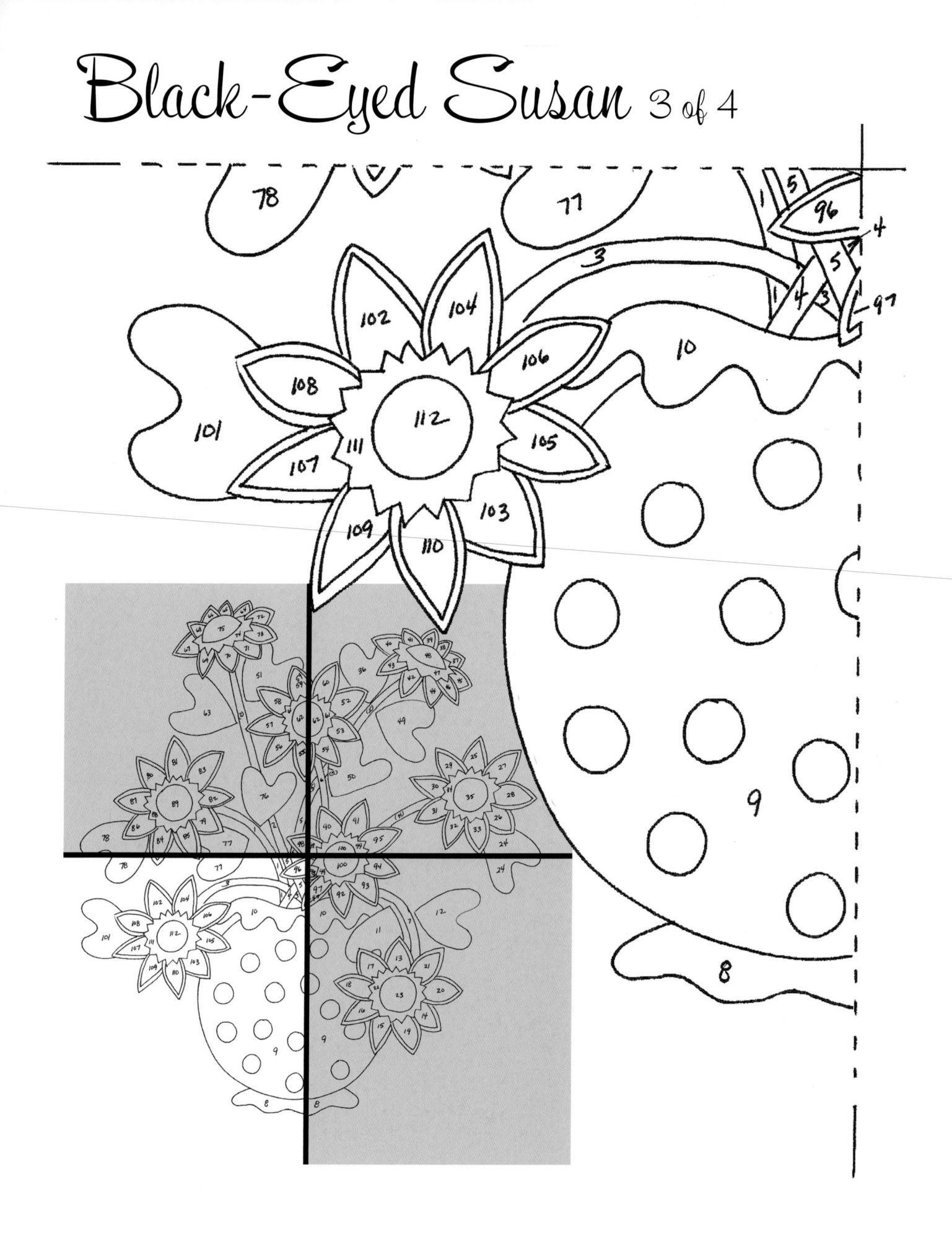

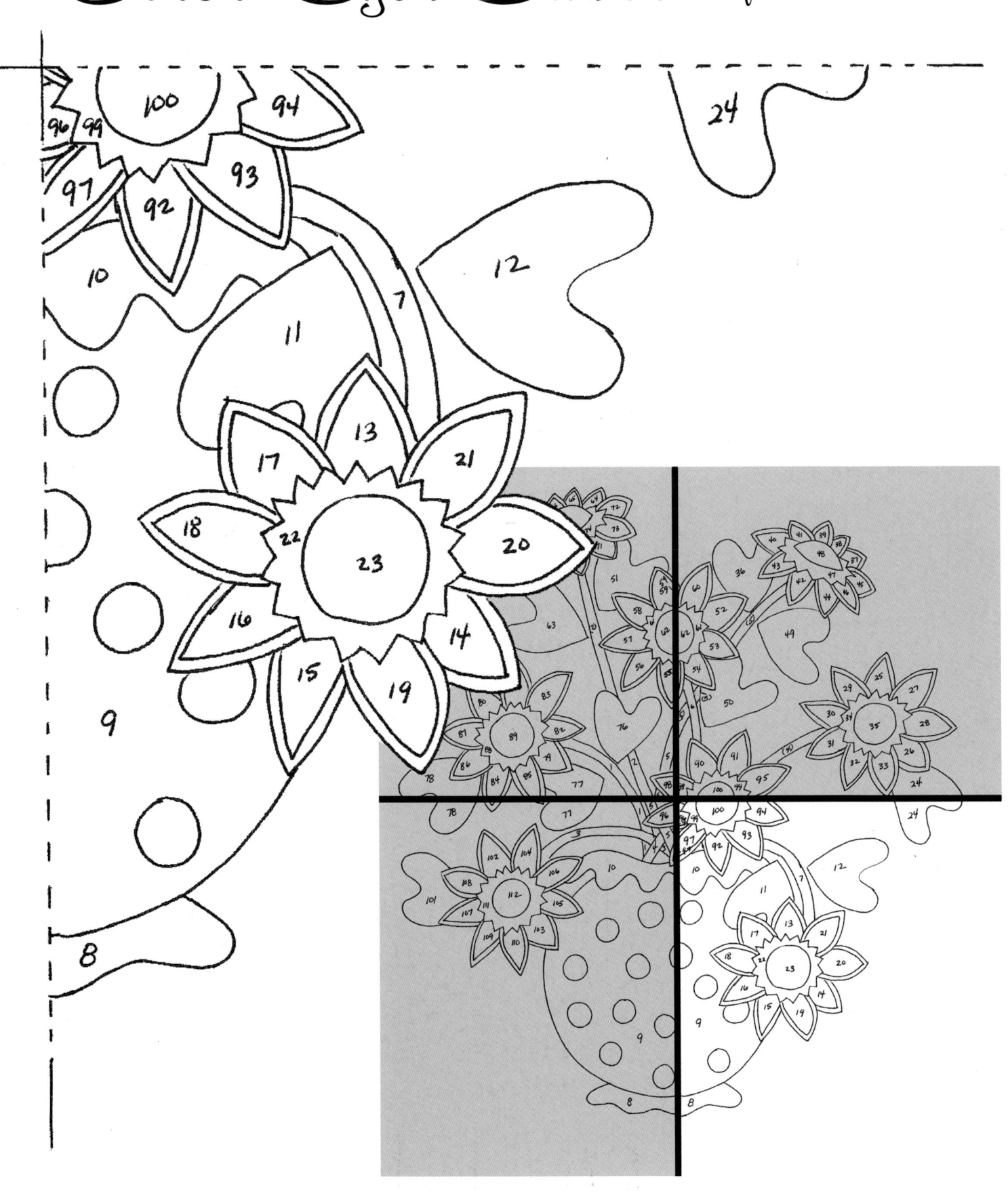

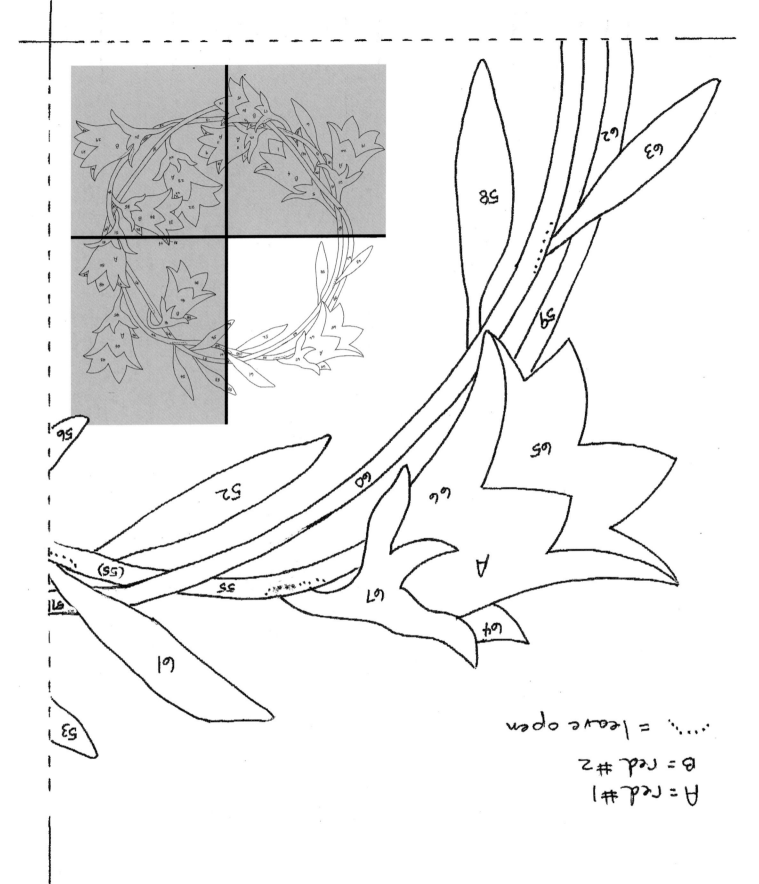

A = red #1
B = red #2
·····: = leave open

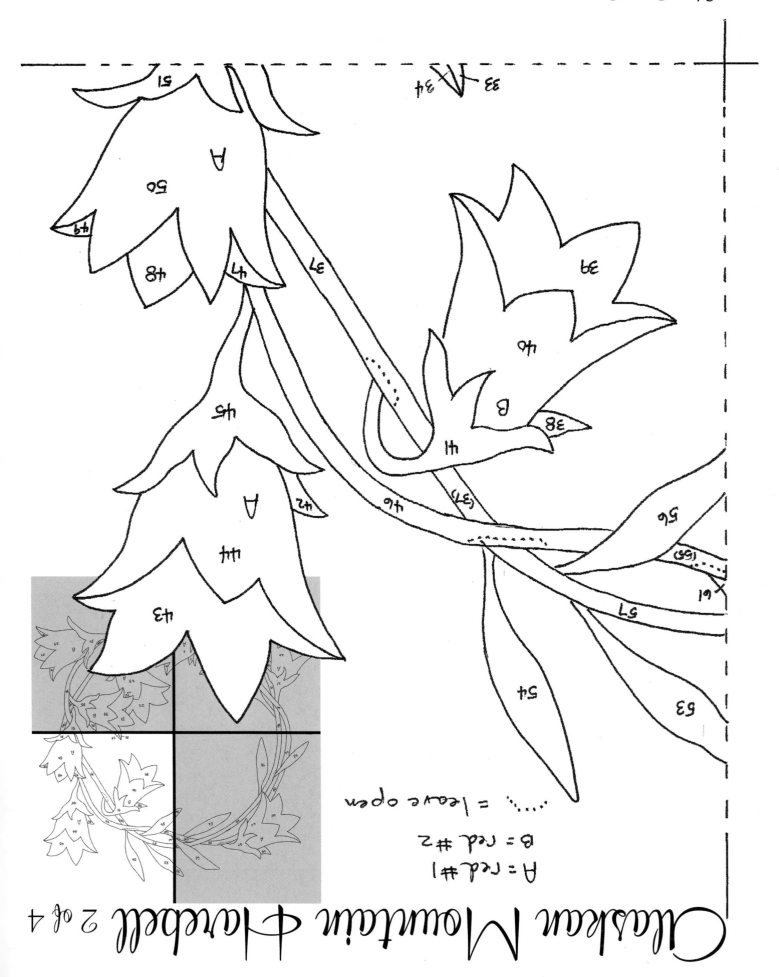

Alaskan Mountain Harebell 2 of 4

A = red #1
B = red #2

⋯⋯ = leave open

A = red #1
B = red #2
..... = leave open

Alaskan Mountain Harebell 3 of 4

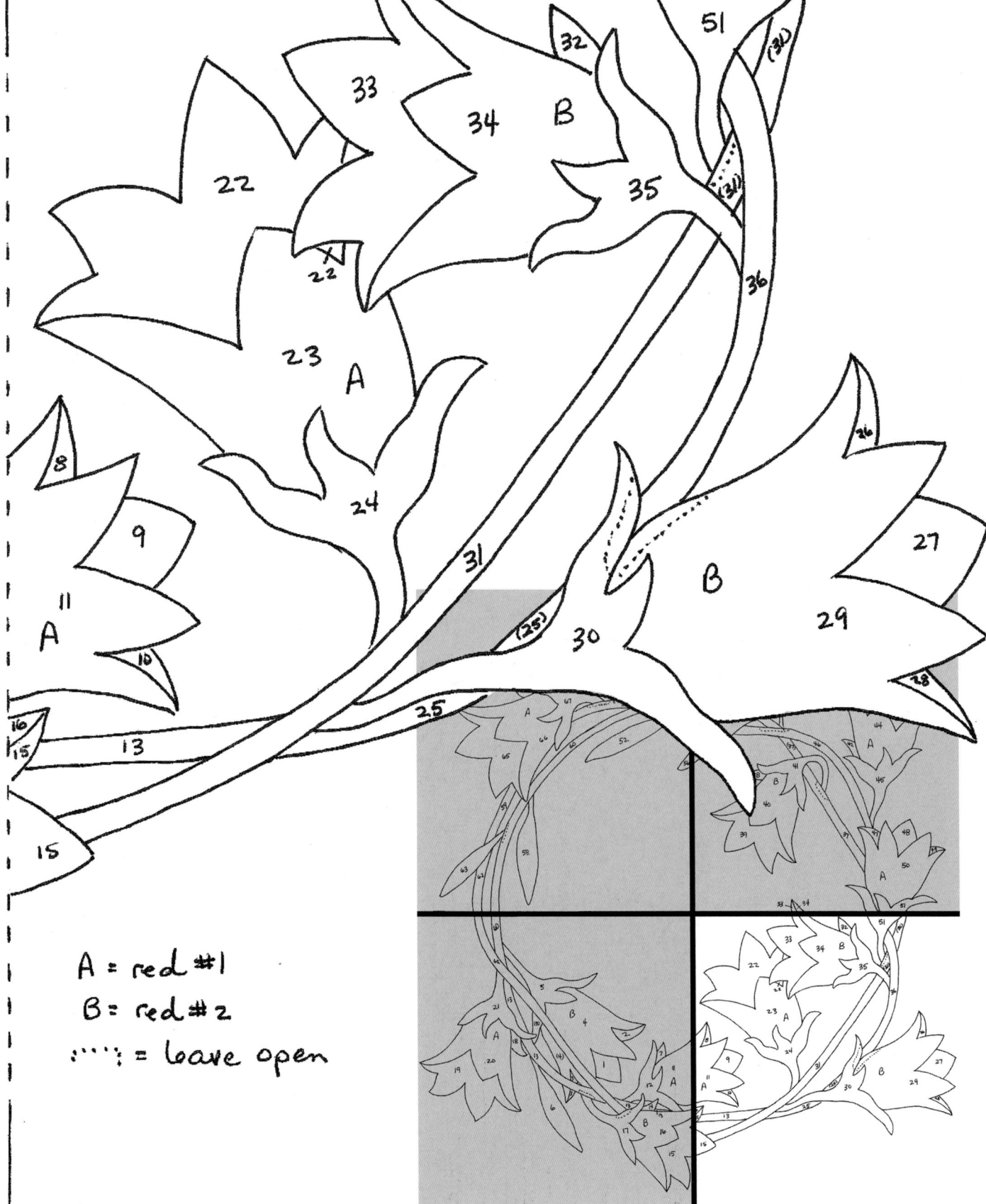

A = red #1
B = red #2
·····: = leave open

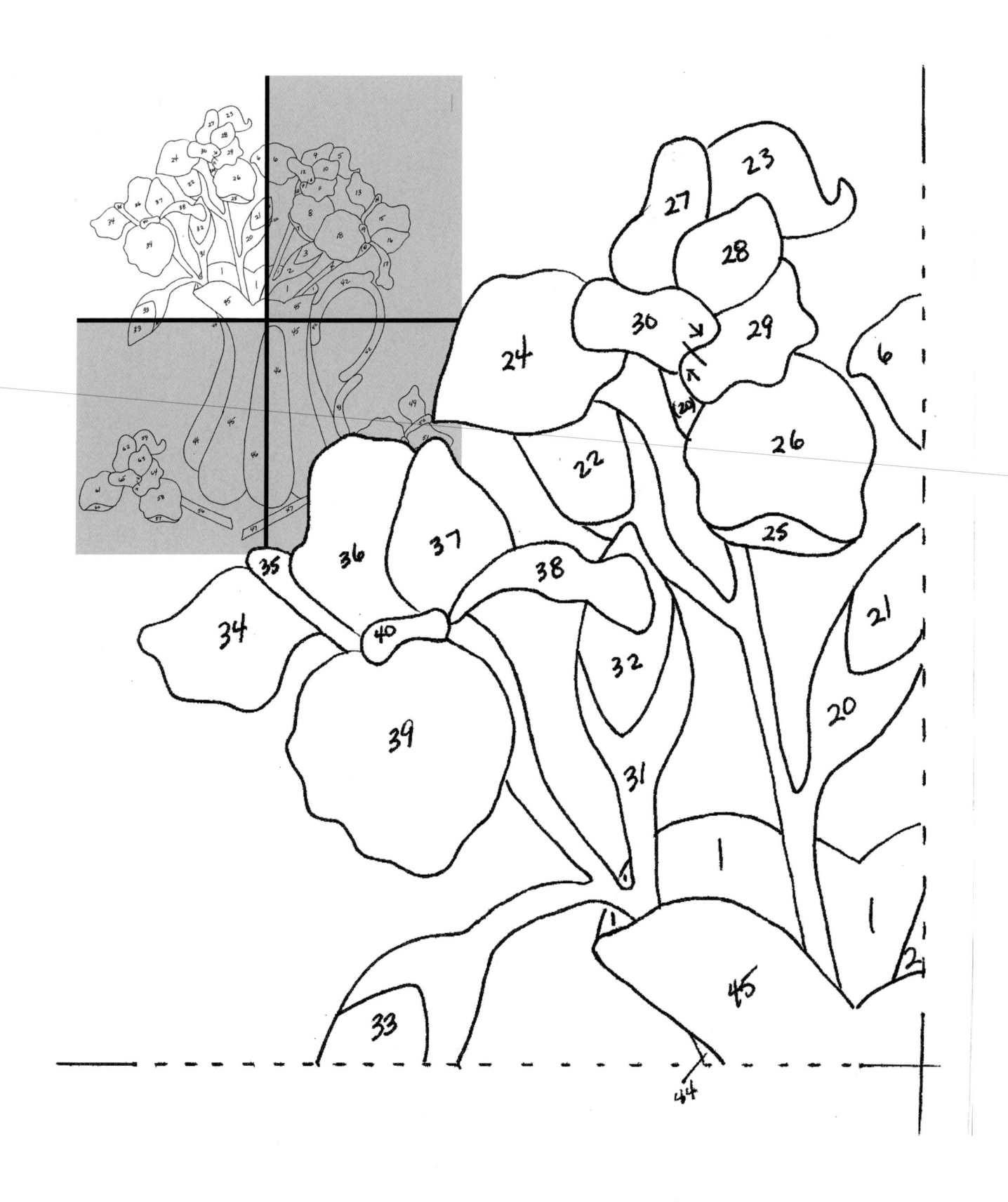

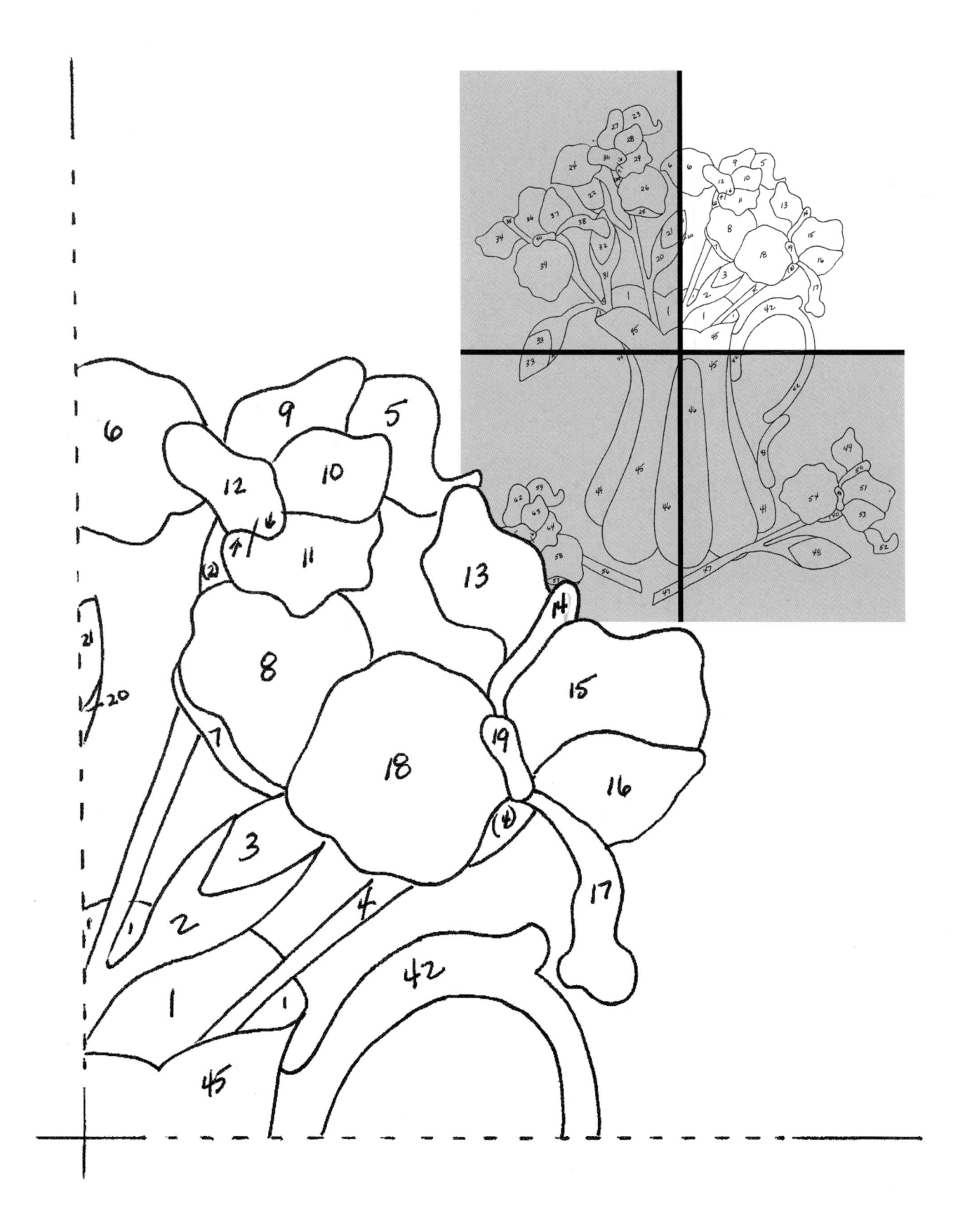

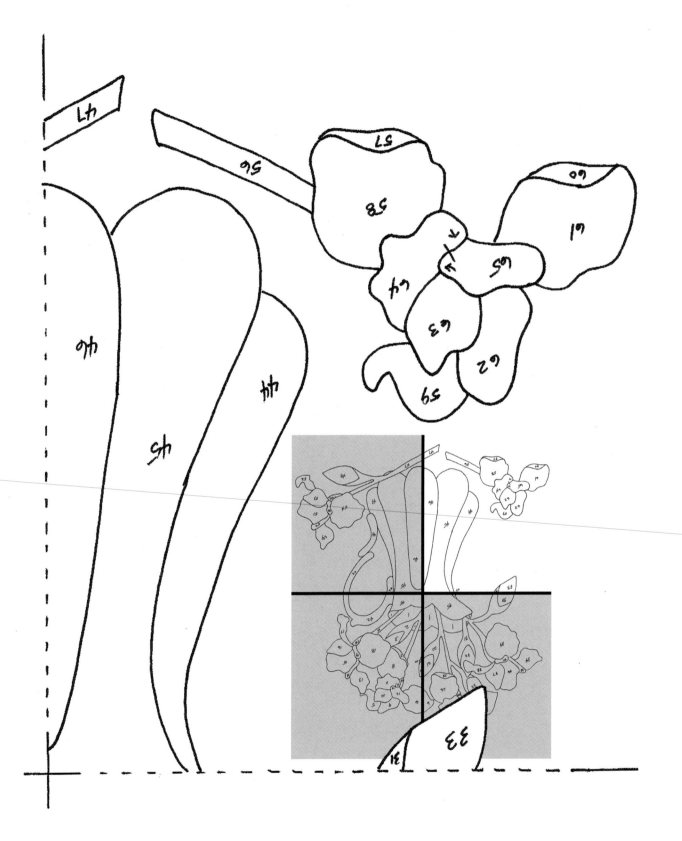

47

56

57

58

60

61

67

65

63

62

59

46

45

44

Grils 3 of 4

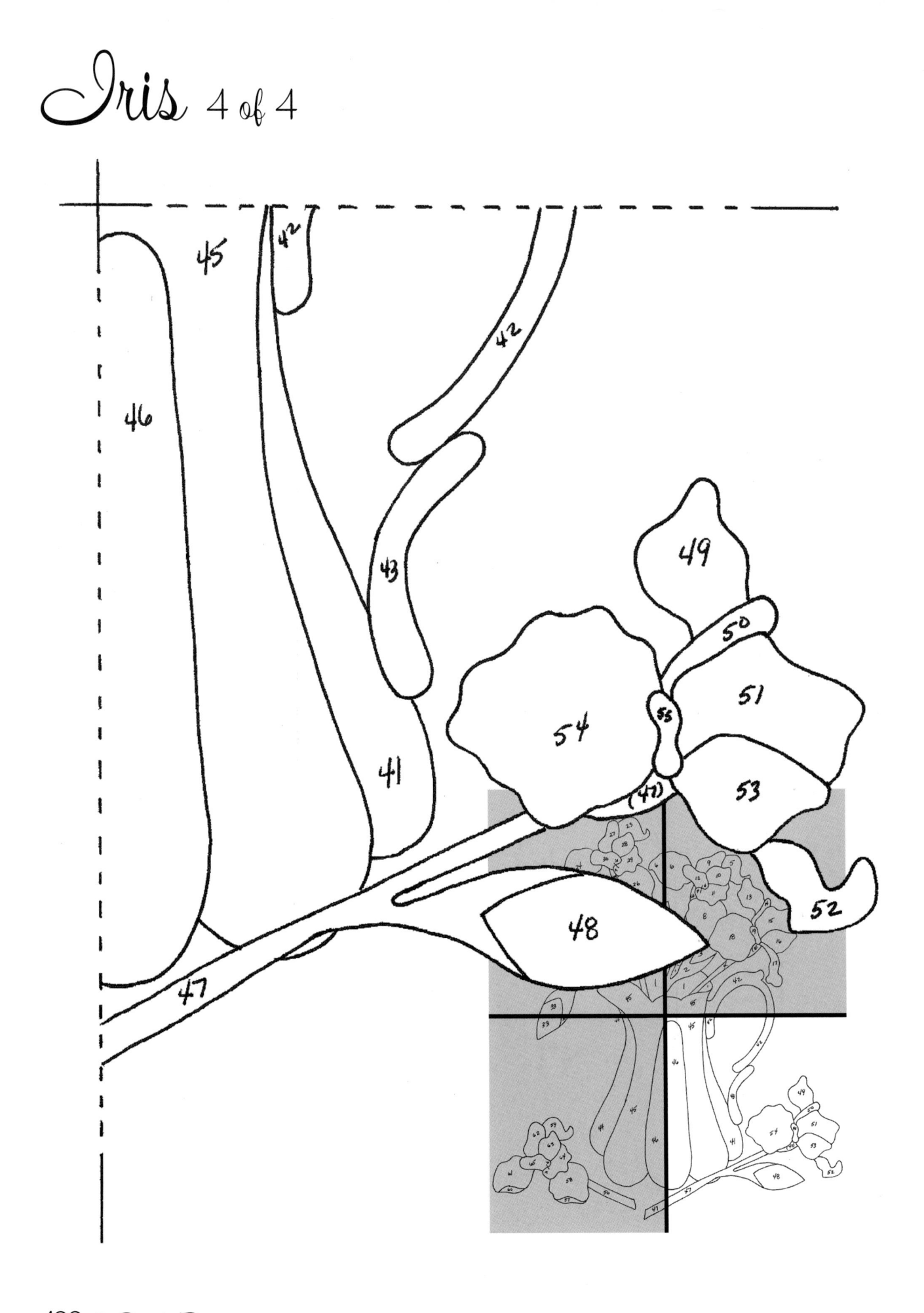

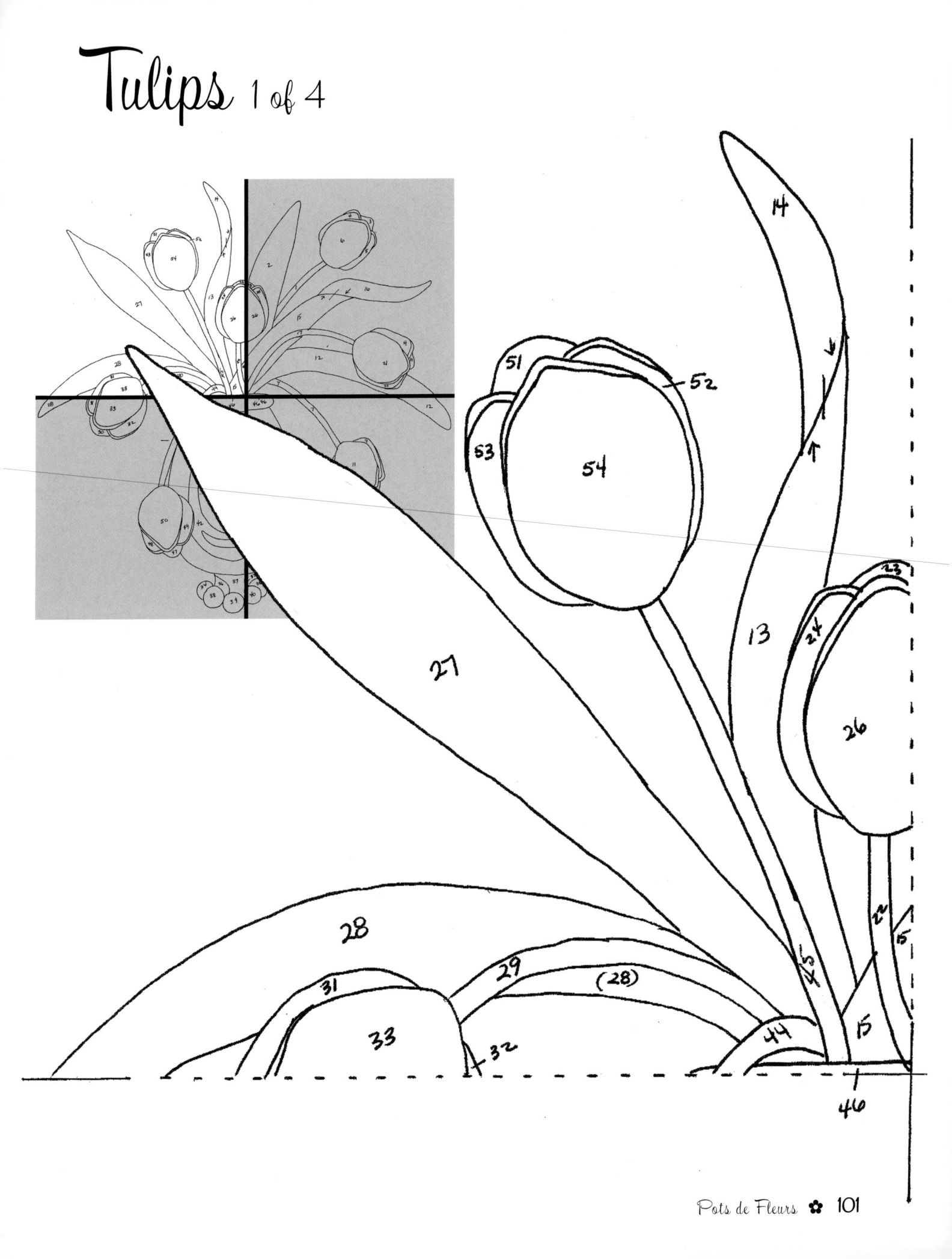

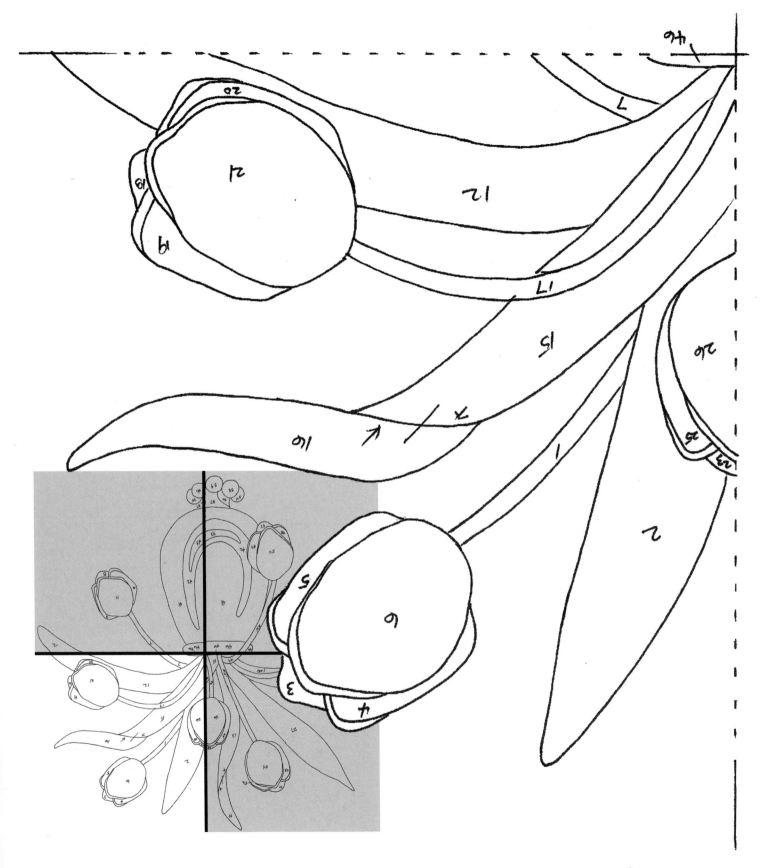

Tulips 2 of 4

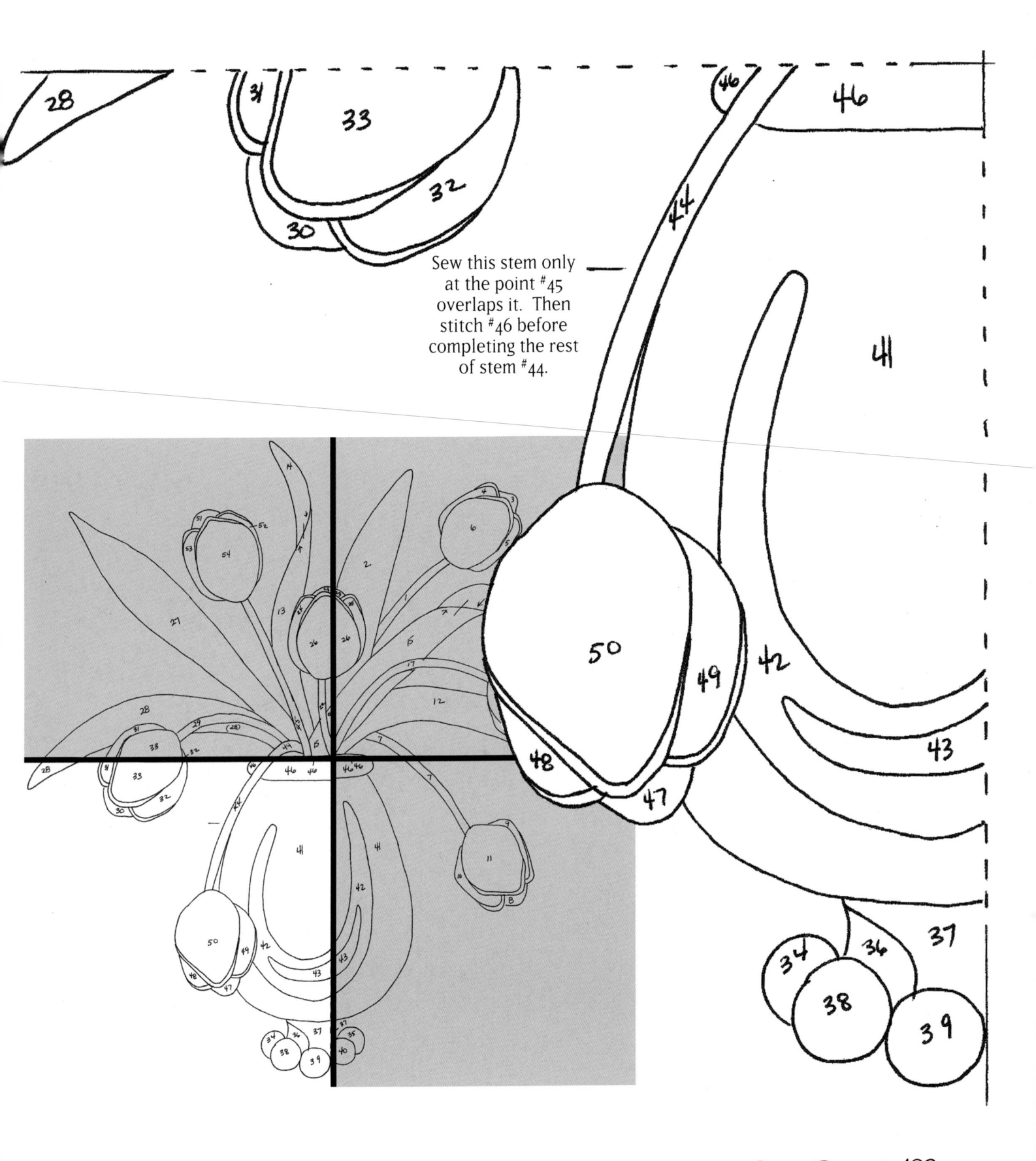

Sew this stem only
at the point #45
overlaps it. Then
stitch #46 before
completing the rest
of stem #44.

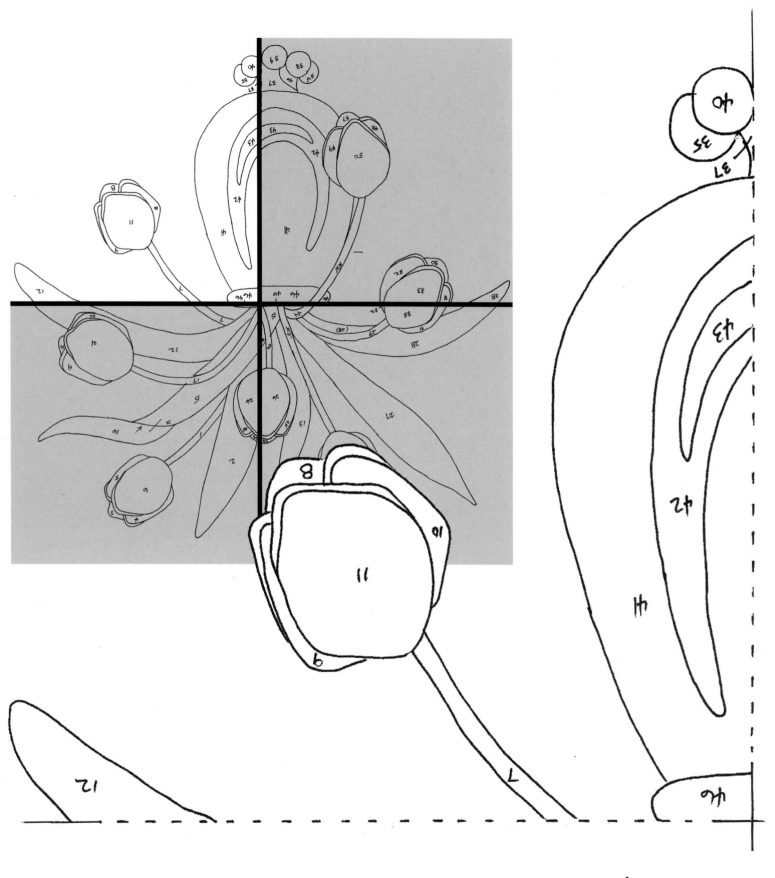

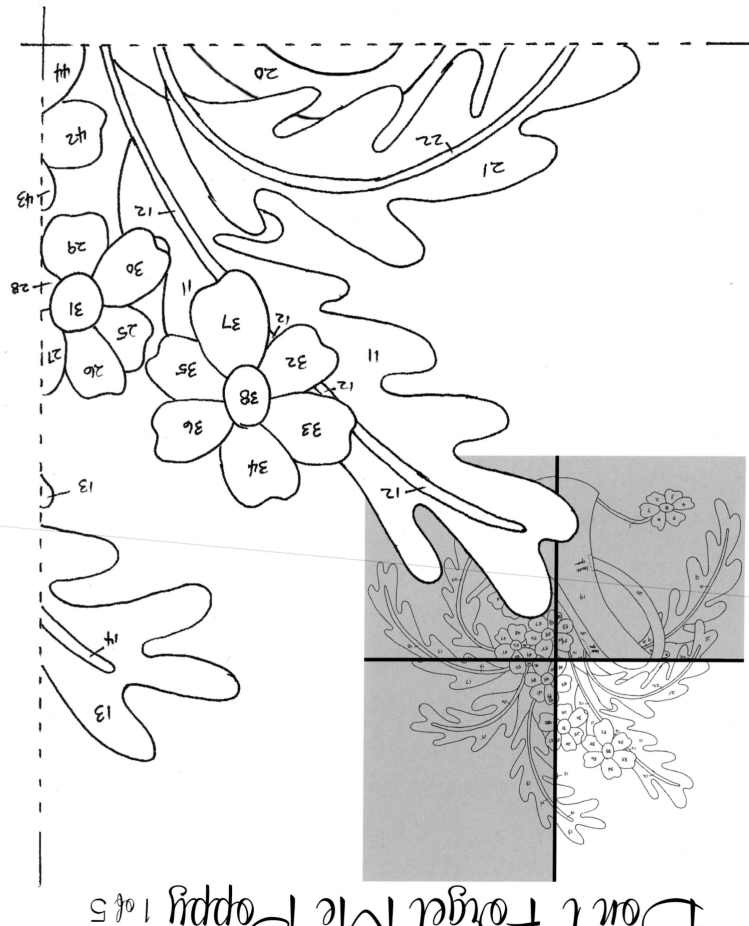

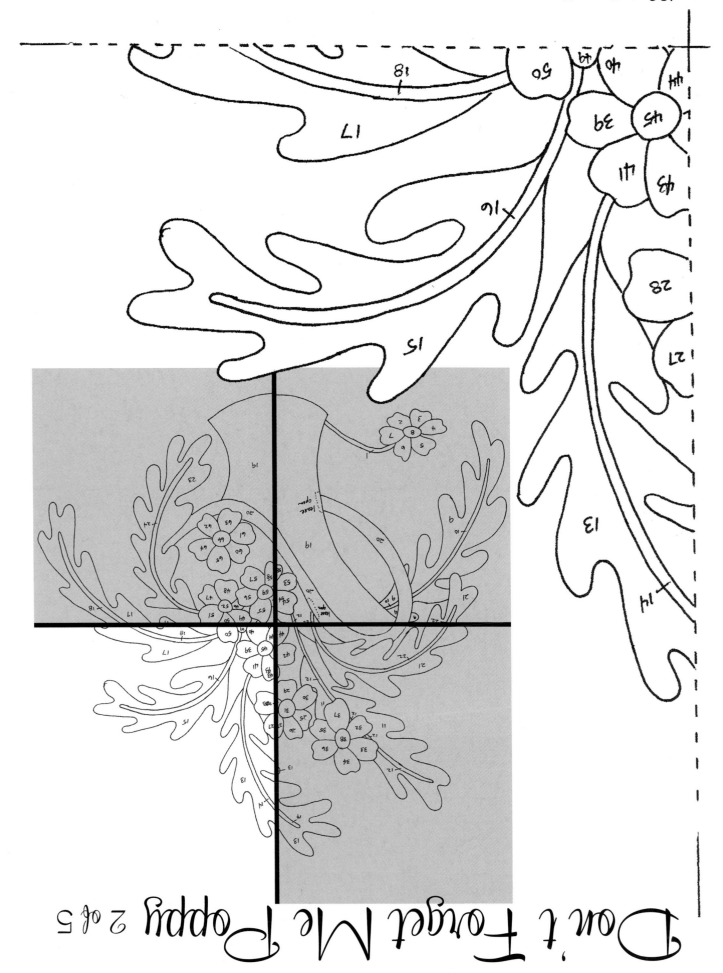

Don't Forget Me Poppy 2 of 5

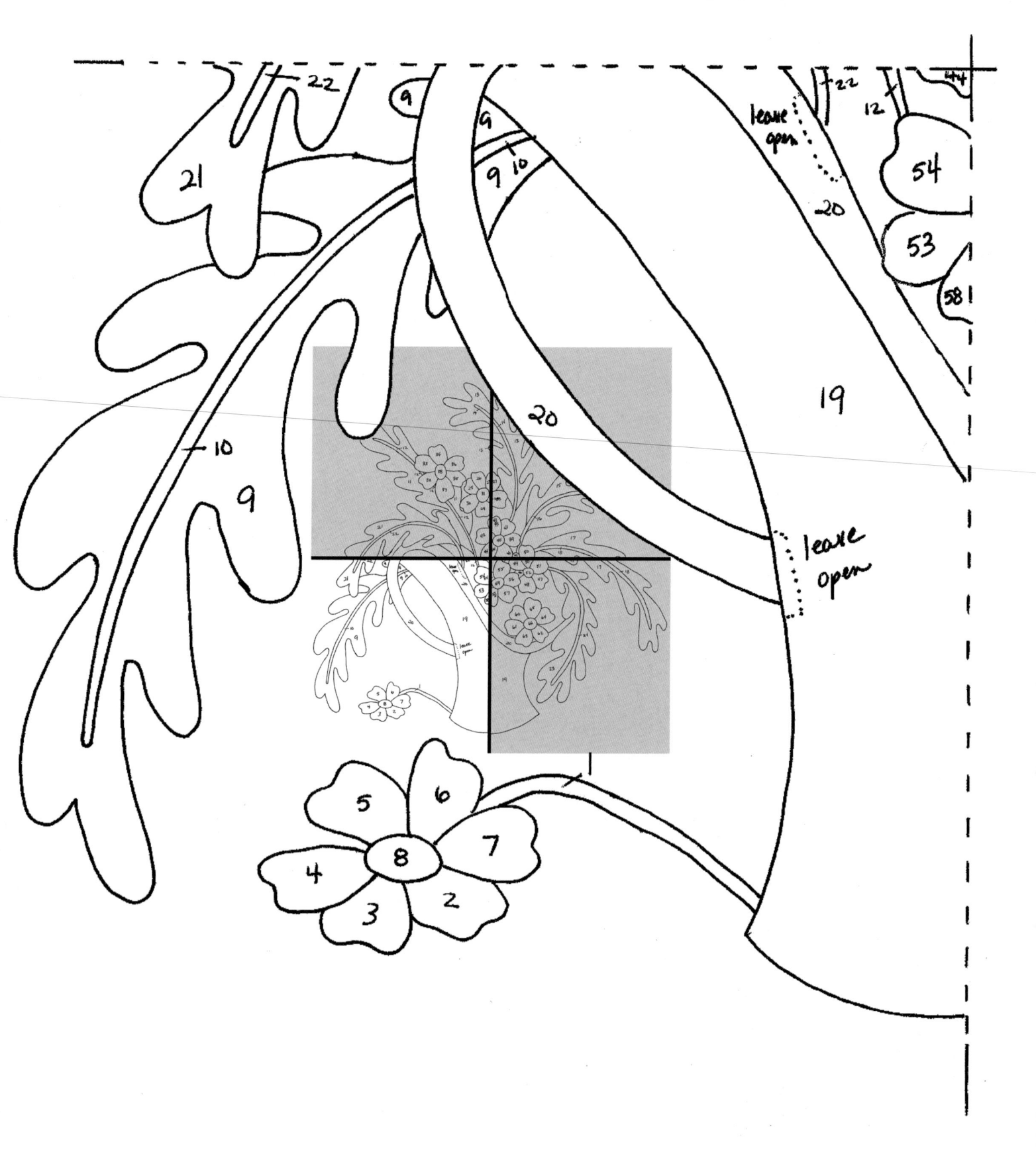

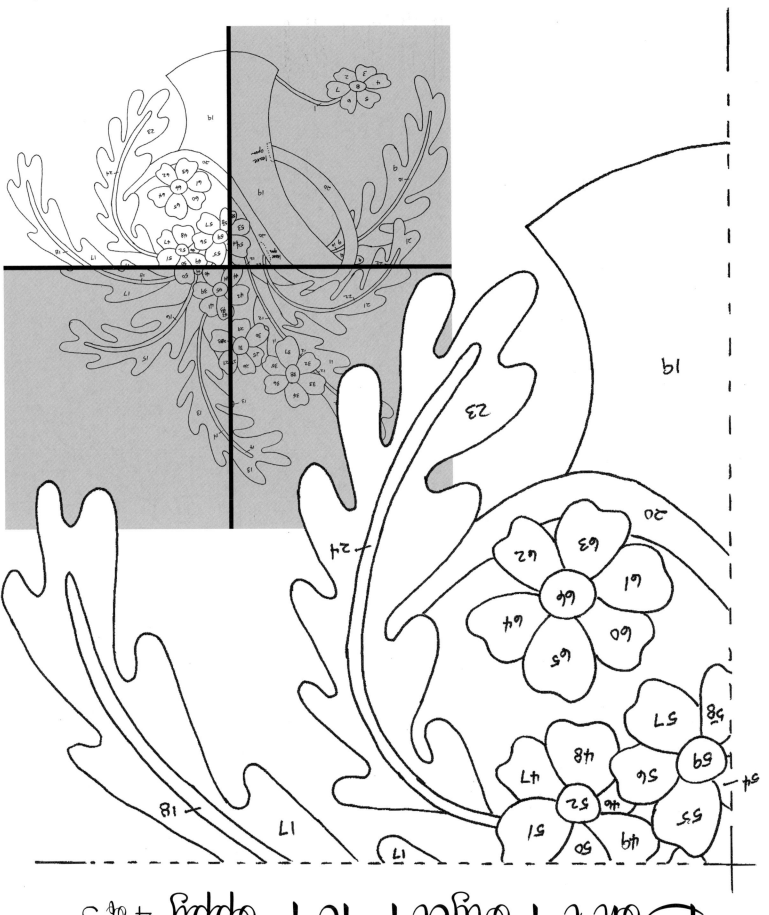

Don't Forget Me Poppy 4 of 5

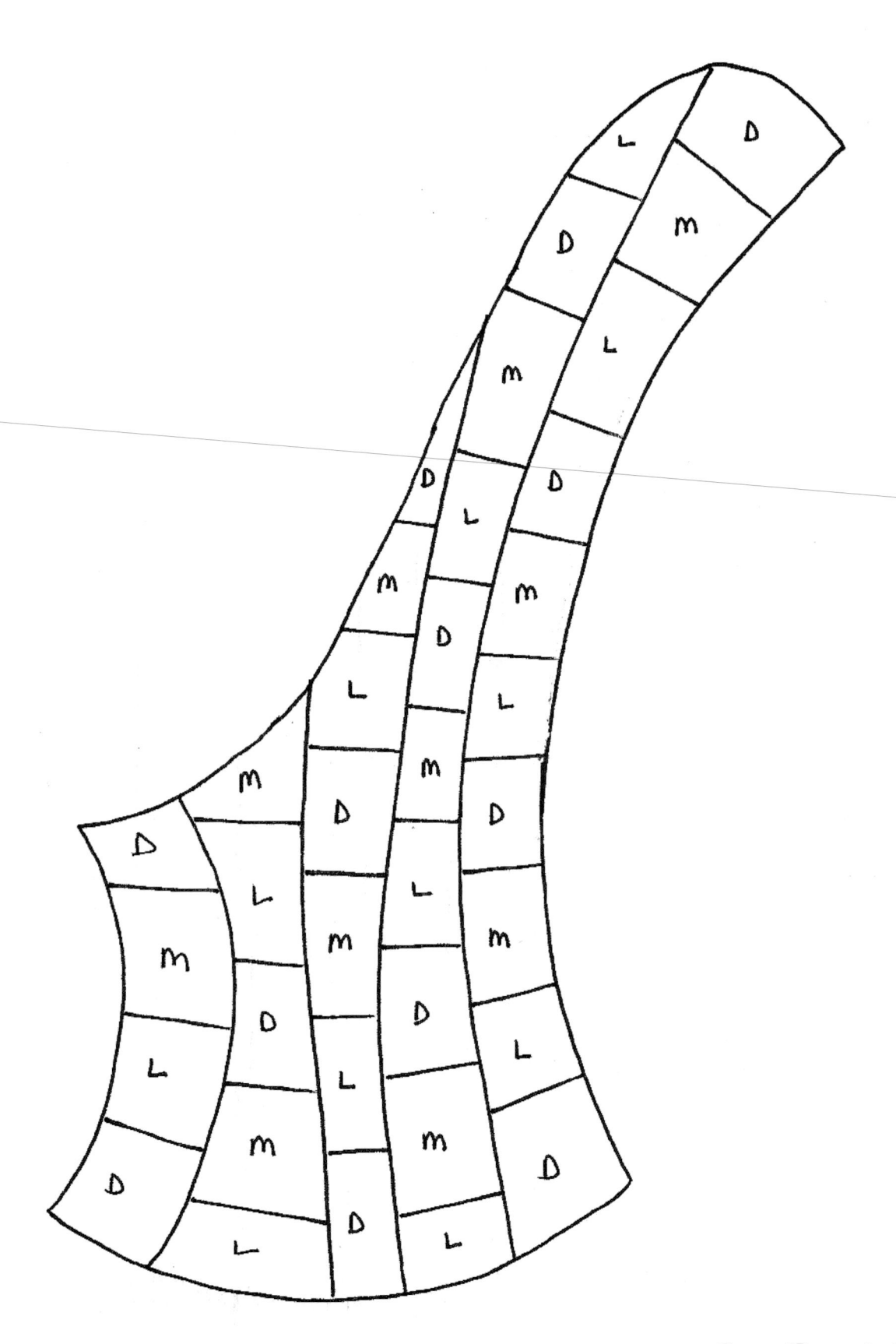

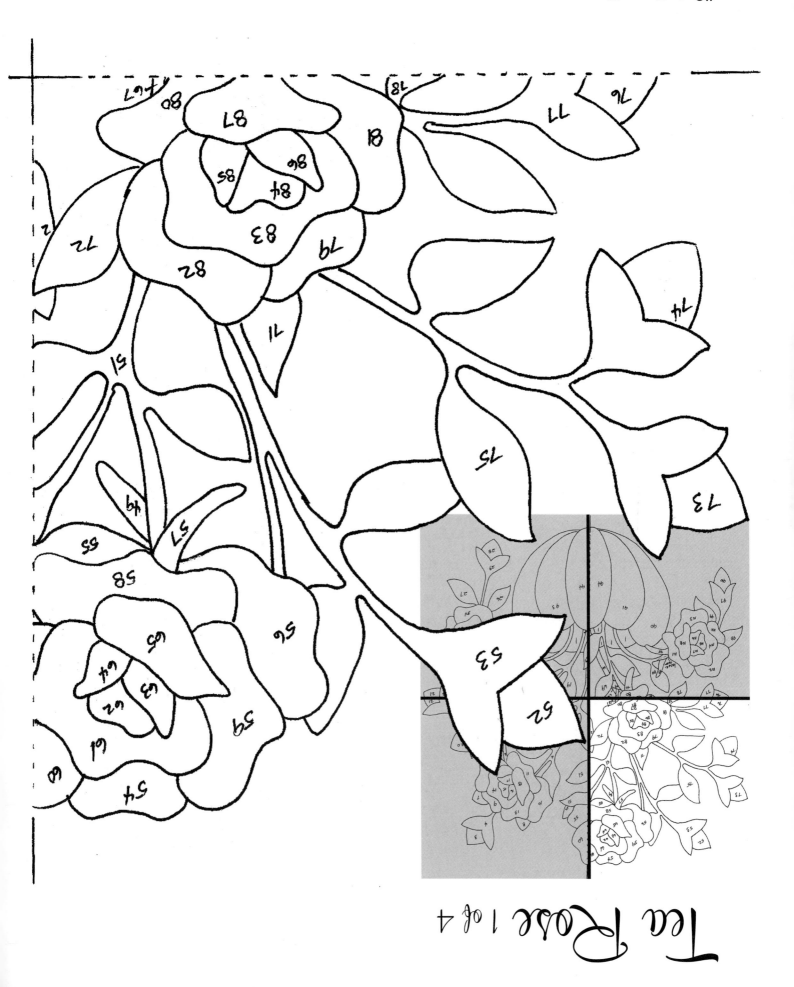

Tea Rose 1 of 4

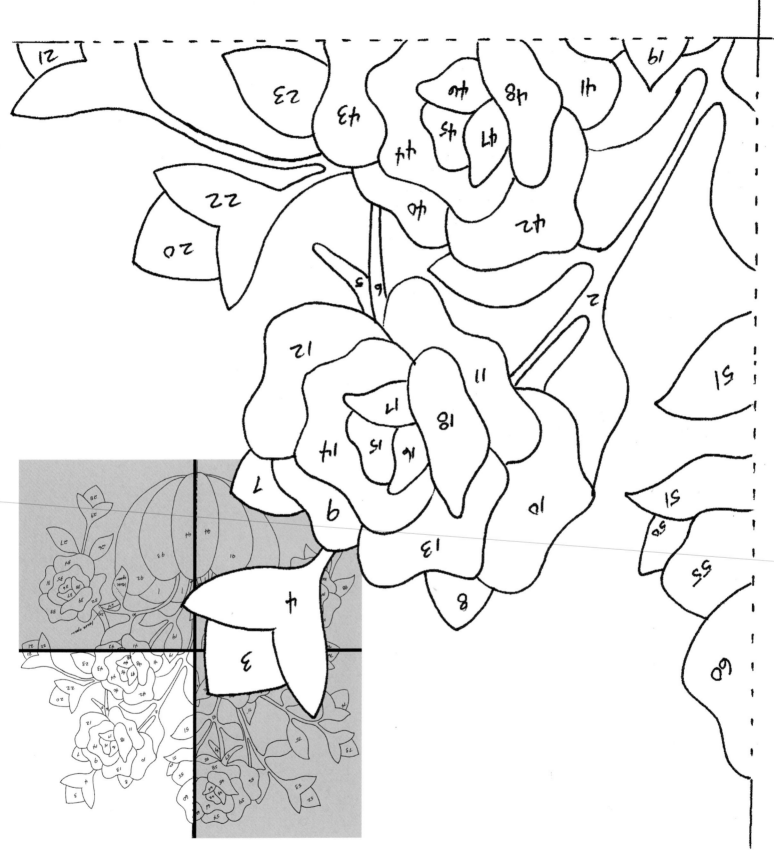

Tea Rose 2 of 4

Piece #1 is just one piece, not eight. Cut piece #66 as one.

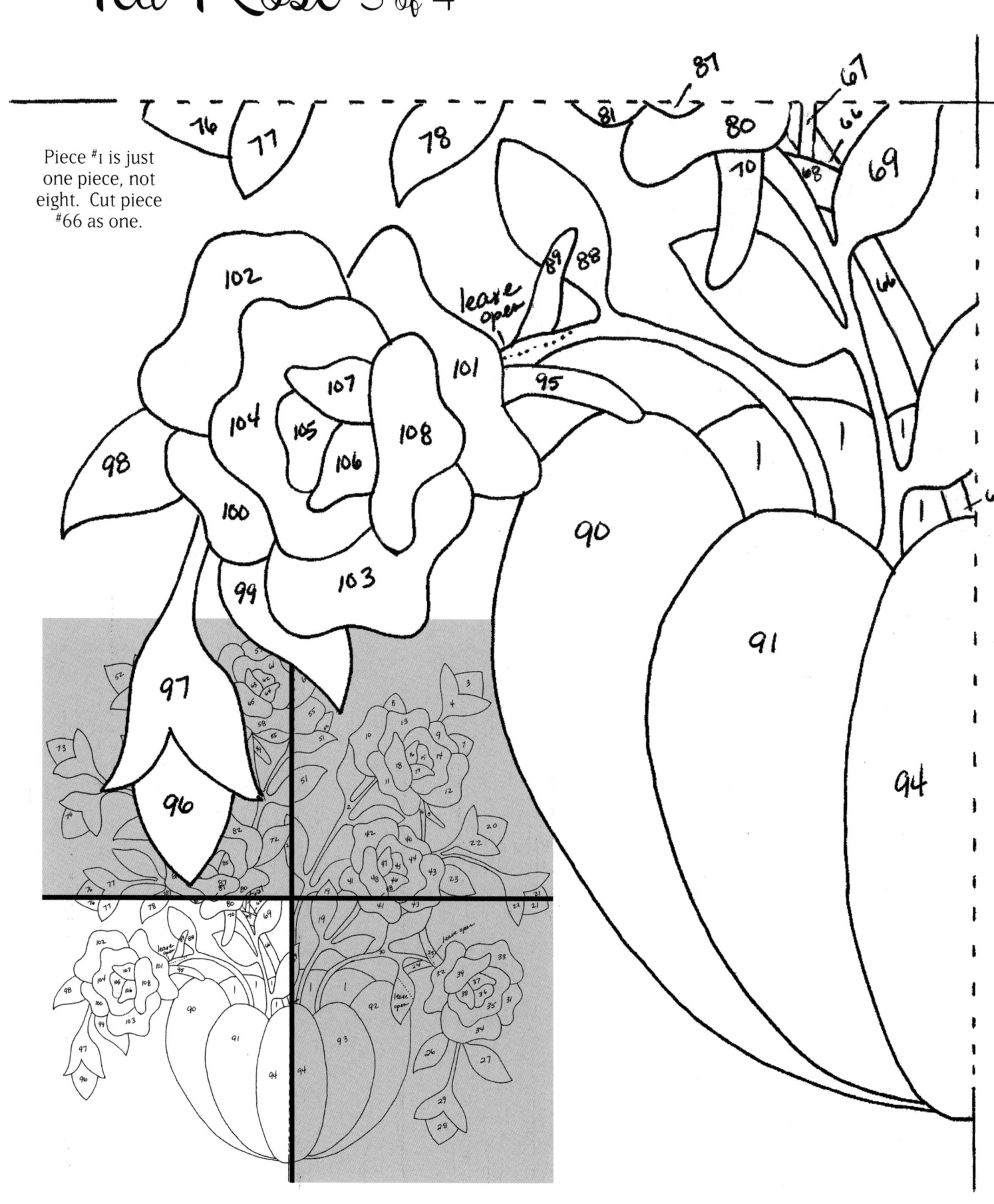

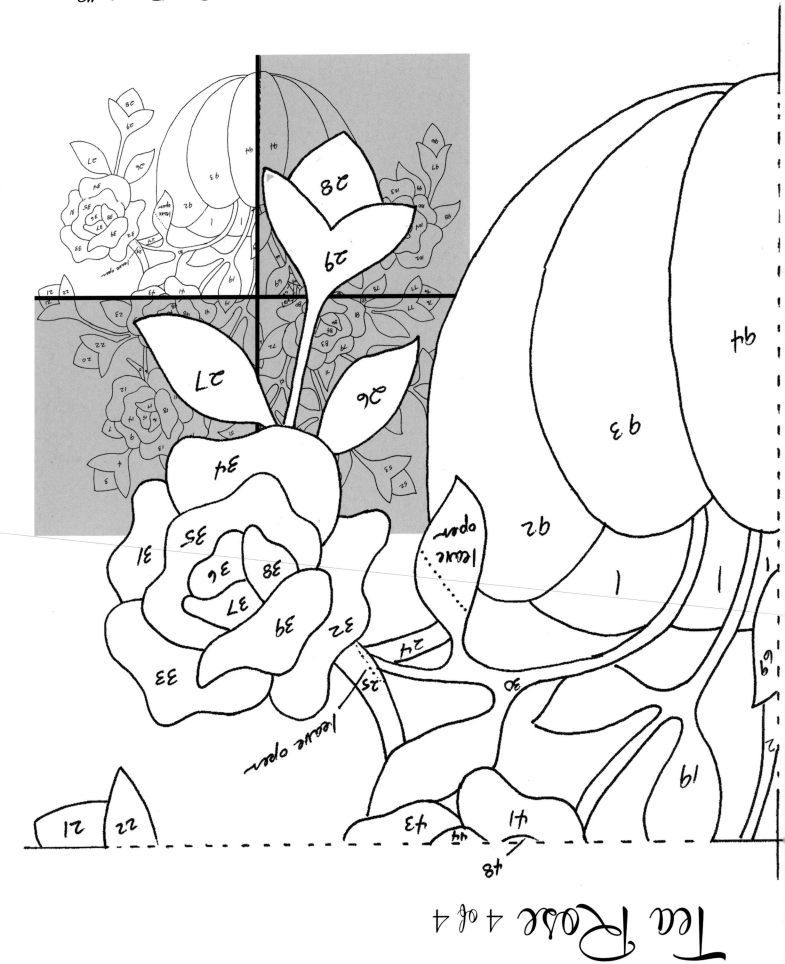

Tea Rose 4 of 4

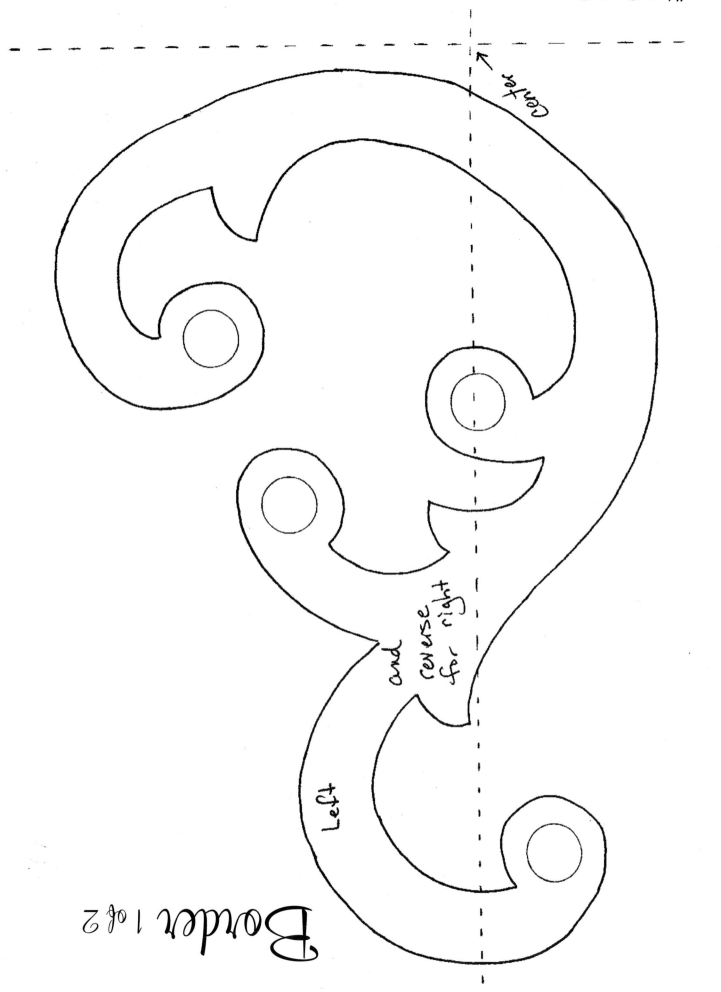

Center

reverse
for right

and

Left

Border 1 of 2

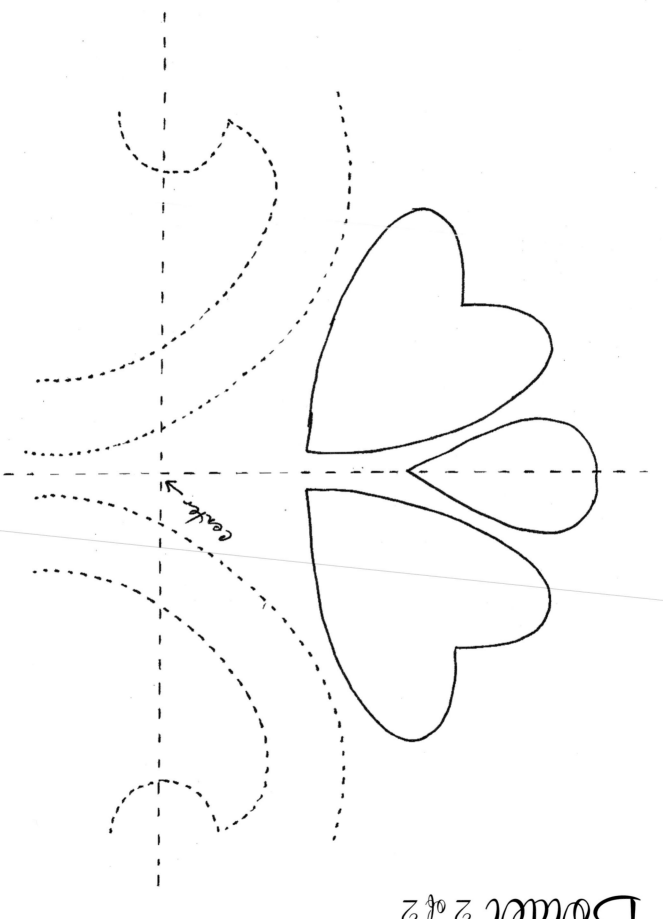

Border 2 of 2

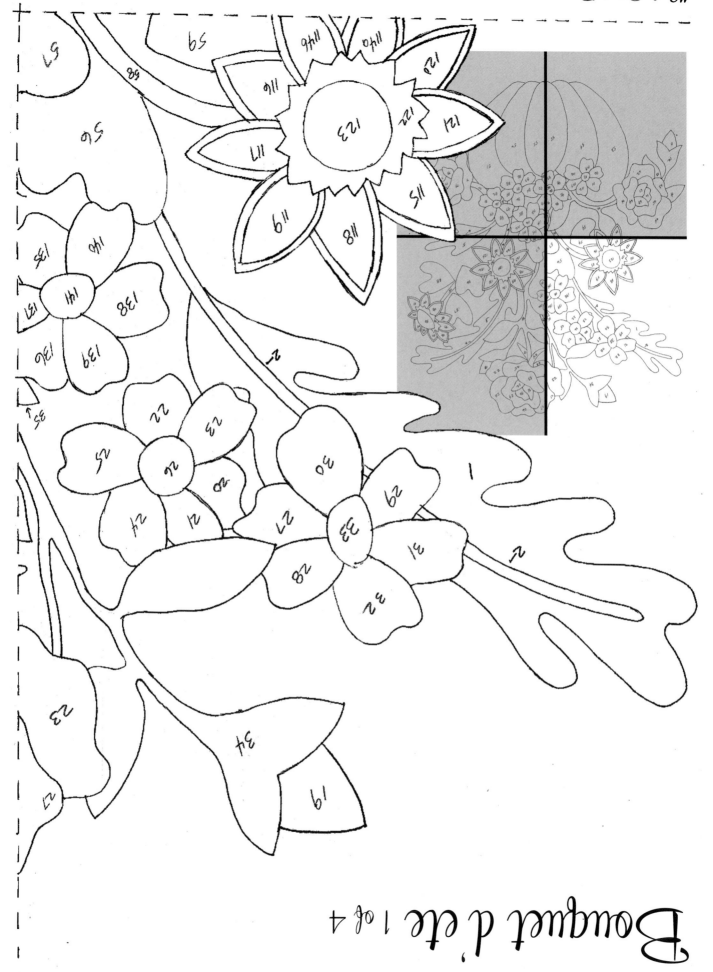

Bouquet d'été 1 of 4

Bouquet d'été 2 of 4

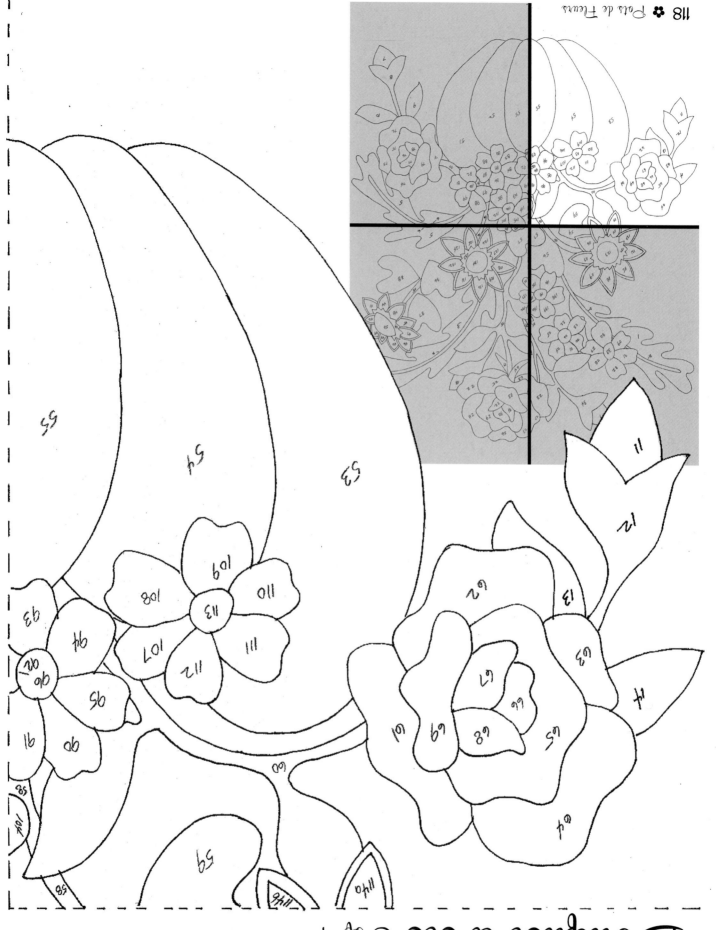

Bouquet d'été 4 of 4

Other Star Quilt Books:

One Piece at a Time by Kansas City Star Books — 1999

More Kansas City Star Quilts by Kansas City Star Books — 2000

Outside the Box: Hexagon Patterns from The Kansas City Star by Edie McGinnis — 2001

Prairie Flower: A Year on the Plains by Barbara Brackman — 2001

The Sister Blocks by Edie McGinnis — 2001

Kansas City Quiltmakers by Doug Worgul — 2001

O' Glory: Americana Quilts Blocks from The Kansas City Star by Edie McGinnis — 2001

Hearts and Flowers: Hand Appliqué from Start to Finish by Kathy Delaney — 2002

Roads and Curves Ahead: A Trip Through Time with Classic Kansas City Star Quilt Blocks by Edie McGinnis — 2002

Celebration of American Life: Appliqué Patterns Honoring a Nation and Its People by Barb Adams and Alma Allen — 2002

Women of Grace & Charm: A Quilting Tribute to the Women Who Served in World War II by Barb Adams and Alma Allen — 2003

A Heartland Album: More Techniques in Hand Appliqué by Kathy Delaney — 2003

Quilting a Poem: Designs Inspired by America's Poets by Frances Kite and Deb Rowden — 2003

Carolyn's Paper Pieced Garden: Patterns for Miniature and Full-Sized Quilts by Carolyn Cullinan McCormick — 2003

Friendships in Bloom: Round Robin Quilts by Marjorie Nelson and Rebecca Nelson-Zerfas — 2003

Baskets of Treasures: Designs Inspired by Life Along the River by Edie McGinnis — 2003

Heart & Home: Unique American Women and the Houses that Inspire by Kathy Schmitz — 2003

Women of Design: Quilts in the Newspaper by Barbara Brackman — 2004

The Basics: An Easy Guide to Beginning Quiltmaking by Kathy Delaney — 2004

Four Block Quilts: Echoes of History, Pieced Boldly & Appliquéd Freely by Terry Clothier Thompson — 2004

No Boundaries: Bringing Your Fabric Over the Edge by Edie McGinnis — 2004

Horn of Plenty for a New Century by Kathy Delaney — 2004

Quilting the Garden by Barb Adams and Alma Allen — 2004

Stars All Around Us: Quilts and Projects Inspired by a Beloved Symbol by Cherie Ralston — 2005

Quilters' Stories: Collecting History in the Heart of America by Deb Rowden — 2005

Libertyville: Where Liberty Dwells, There is My Country by Terry Clothier Thompson — 2005

Sparkling Jewels, Pearls of Wisdom by Edie McGinnis — 2005

Grapefruit Juice and Sugar: Bold Quilts Inspired by Grandmother's Legacy by Jenifer Dick — 2005

Home Sweet Home by Barb Adams and Alma Allen — 2005

Patterns of History: The Challenge Winners by Kathy Delaney — 2005

My Quilt Stories by Debra Rowden — 2005

Quilts in Red and Green and the Women Who Made Them by Nancy Hornback and Terry Clothier Thompson — 2006

Hard Times, Splendid Quilts: A 1930s Celebration, Paper Piecing from The Kansas City Star by Carolyn Cullinan McCormick — 2006

Art Nouveau Quilts for the 21st Century by Bea Oglesby — 2006

Designer Quilts: Great Projects from Moda's Best Fabric Artists — 2006

Birds of a Feather by Barb Adams and Alma Allen — 2006

Feedsacks! Beautiful Quilts from Humble Beginnings by Edie McGinnis — 2006

Kansas Spirit: Historical Quilt Blocks and the Saga of the Sunflower State by Jeanne Poore — 2006

Bold Improvisation: Searching for African-American Quilts — The Heffley Collection by Scott Heffley — 2007

The Soulful Art of African-American Quilts: Nineteen Bold, Improvisational Projects by Sonie Ruffin — 2007

Alphabet Quilts: Letters for All Ages by Bea Oglesby — 2007

Beyond the Basics: A Potpourri of Quiltmaking Techniques by Kathy Delaney — 2007

Golden's Journal: 20 Sampler Blocks Honoring Prairie Farm Life by Christina DeArmond, Eula Lang and Kaye Spitzli — 2007

Borderland in Butternut and Blue: A Sampler Quilt to Recall the Civil War Along the Kansas/Missouri Border by Barbara Brackman — 2007

Come to the Fair: Quilts that Celebrate State Fair Traditions by Edie McGinnis — 2007

Cotton and Wool: Miss Jump's Farewell by Linda Brannock — 2007

You're Invited! Quilts and Homes to Inspire by Barb Adams and Alma Allen, Blackbird Designs — 2007

Portable Patchwork: Who Says You Can't Take it With You? by Donna Thomas — 2008

Quilts for Rosie: Paper Piecing Patterns from the '40s by Carolyn Cullinan McCormick — 2008

Fruit Salad: Appliqué Designs for Delicious Quilts by Bea Oglesby — 2008

Red, Green and Beyond by Nancy Hornback and Terry Clothier Thompson — 2008

A Dusty Garden Grows by Terry Clothier Thompson — 2008

We Gather Together: A Harvest of Quilts by Jan Patek — 2008

With These Hands: 19th Century-Inspired Primitive Projects for Your Home by Maggie Bonanomi — 2008

As the Cold Wind Blows by Barb Adams and Alma Allen — 2008

Caring for Your Quilts: Textile Conservation, Repair and Storage by Hallye Bone — 2008

The Circuit Rider's Quilt: An Album Quilt Honoring a Beloved Minister by Jenifer Dick — 2008

Embroidered Quilts: From Hands and Hearts by Christina DeArmond, Eula Lang and Kaye Spitzli — 2008

Reminiscing: A Whimsicals Collections by Terri Degenkolb — 2008

Scraps and Shirttails: Reuse, Re-purpose and Recycle! The Art of Green Quilting by Bonnie Hunter — 2008

Flora Botanica: Quilts from the Spencer Museum of Art by Barbara Brackman — 2009

Making Memories: Simple Quilts from Cherished Clothing by Deb Rowden — 2009

Pots de Fleurs: A Garden of Applique Techniques by Kathy Delaney — 2009

Wedding Ring, Pickle Dish and More: Paper Piecing Curves by Carolyn McCormick - 2009

Queen Bees Mysteries:

Murders on Elderberry Road by Sally Goldenbaum — 2003

A Murder of Taste by Sally Goldenbaum — 2004

Murder on a Starry Night by Sally Goldenbaum — 2005

Dog-Gone Murder by Marnette Falley — 2008

Project Books:

Fan Quilt Memories by Jeanne Poore — 2000

Santa's Parade of Nursery Rhymes by Jeanne Poore — 2001

As the Crow Flies by Edie McGinnis — 2007

Sweet Inspirations by Pam Manning — 2007

Quilts Through the Camera's Eye by Terry Clothier Thompson — 2007

Louisa May Alcott: Quilts of Her Life, Her Work, Her Heart by Terry Clothier Thompson — 2008

The Lincoln Museum Quilt: A Reproduction for Abe's Frontier Cabin by Barbara Brackman and Deb Rowden — 2008

Dinosaurs - Stomp, Chomp and Roar by Pam Manning — 2008

Carrie Hall's Sampler: Favorite Blocks from a Classic Pattern Collection by Barbara Brackman — 2008

Just Desserts: Quick Quilts Using Pre-cut Fabrics by Edie McGinnis - 2009

DVD Projects:

The Kansas City Stars: A Quilting Legacy — 2008

Resources:

Aurofil cotton thread — www.thatthreadshop.com

Clover Silk thread, Mechanical Pencil, White Pen, appliqué pins —
  www.clover-usa.com

Mettler cotton thread — available at sewing centers everywhere

DMC cotton thread — www.dmc-usa.com

Kinkame Silk thread — www.unitednotions.com

Colonial needles, Richard Hemming needles, John James needles -
  www.colonialneedle.com

Bohin needles and marker — available at many quilt shops

Jeana Kimball needles — www.jeanakimballquilter.com

Ghinger scissors — available in most sewing centers and quilt shops

Dovo scissors — available in many quilt shops

Fiskars scissors — www.fiskars.com

Soapstone marker — available at many quilt shops

Omnigrid rulers — available at sewing centers and quilt shops
  everywhere

Perfect Circles by Karen Kay Buckley — www.karenkaybuckley.com

Add-a-Quarter Ruler — CM Designs; available at most quilt shops

Notes: